SONGBOOK

SONGBOOK

Selected Poems

by Umberto Saba

Selected, Translated and Introduced
by Stephen Sartarelli

The Sheep Meadow Press
Riverdale-on-Hudson, New York

Translation copyright © 1998 by Stephen Sartarelli
Introduction copyright © 1998 by Stephen Sartarelli

The material in this book was originally published in *Il Canzoniere*, © 1981 by Arnaldo Mondadori Editore.

All inquiries and permission requests should be addressed to:
The Sheep Meadow Press
PO Box 1345
Riverdale-on-Hudson, New York 10471.

Printed on acid-free paper in the United States. This book meets the guidelines for permanence and durability of the Committee on Production Guidelines for Book Longevity of the Council on Library Resources.

Cover: Giorgio Morandi, etching.

Library of Congress Cataloging-in-Publication Data

Saba, Umberto, 1883-1957
     [Canzoniere. English & Italian. Selections]
     Songbook: Selected Poems / by Umberto Saba; selected, translated and introduced by Stephen Sartarelli.
          p.   cm.
     English and Italian.
     Includes bibliographical references.
     ISBN 1-878818-52-X (pbk. : alk. paper)
     1. Saba, Umberto, 1883–1957—Translations into English.
     I. Sartarelli, Stephen, 1954–   . II. Title.
     PQ4841.A18A25 1998
     851'.912—dc21   98-40946
                                                                    CIP

Distributed by the University Press of New England.

for my two fathers

CONTENTS

from *Mediterranea* (1945-46)

from *Epigraph* (1947-48)

from *Birds* (1948)

from *Almost a Story* (1951)

from *Six Poems of Old Age* (1953-54)

Introduction

Saba the Man, Saba the Poet

As much as any lyric poet in any language, ancient or modern, Umberto Saba fashioned an art in which the life and the work constantly mirror and sustain one another. Of course all lyric poetry, traditionally at least, tends to express subjective experience, whether that of the individual poet or that codified in myth and legend and then given a personal voice by the poet. Love, ambition, spiritual yearning, time and its inexorable passage, the fear of death—such have been the common themes of the lyric mode from Sappho and Catullus to Baudelaire and Robert Duncan, all the modern departures from this norm notwithstanding. Still, there is something in the poetry of Umberto Saba that exceeds even this deep, ancient vein, and has, no doubt, its roots in the personal and general circumstances of his life and formation.

Born Umberto Poli in 1883, Saba came of age at a time when the forms of Western art, and poetry in particular, were in a phase of profound upheaval which has yet, one hundred years later, to complete its cycle. Italian poetry was still dominated by three major figures, whose stars were soon to fall: the flamboyant Gabriele D'Annunzio, decadent poet extraordinaire as well as novelist, pamphleteer and eventually an intrepid middle-aged fighter pilot in World War I; the staid Giosuè Carducci, a neo-Classicist, spokesman of the new Italian liberal bourgeoisie and "civic poet" in the great Italian tradition; and the subdued but original Giovanni Pascoli, whose notion of the poet "as child," and especially his "poetics of objects," were to have a profound influence on the Italian poetry of the 20th century. The *poeti crepuscolari*, the "twilight poets" who offered the banality of everyday life and a general world-weariness as palliatives to both the high rhetoric of D'Annunzio and the academicism of Carducci, were also beginning to emerge on the national scene in the first years of the new century, while the avant-garde experimentalism of the Florence-based group of *La Voce* and the even more radical formalism of the Futurists lay just a few years ahead.

Saba, however, was born and raised in the outlying city of Trieste, sole seaport of the Hapsburg empire until it dissolved in the wake of the first World War. He thus grew up in a doubly provincial city, generally beyond the reach of the major contemporary currents of both Italian and Middle-European culture. It was, as he says in his *History and Chronicle of the Songbook*, still a "Romantic" city, one still living, in the little cultural life it had, "in the time of the Risorgimento." By this he meant two things: that, like all provincial towns, Trieste was years (actually decades) behind the larger trends and thus still embraced Romantic forms of art, literature and music; and that, being a city with an Italian majority still living outside the now unified peninsula, it remained caught in the aspirations, cultural and political, of the age of the Risorgimento, the 50-year political movement for Italian unification which, in its general ideals, was Romantic in nature. These political and cultural facts were to play a large role in Saba's poetic formation.

In such a milieu, Saba notes in the Introduction to his first *Songbook* (*Canzoniere*) of 1921, "nobody spoke to me of good or bad authors." Having, moreover, been forced by his single mother to quit school at age fifteen and find work as a salesman, thus curtailing any chance he might have had to pursue advanced literary studies, he was left utterly alone to fashion for himself what semblance of a literary culture he might find in his remote Mediterranean port, among a population that included Slavs, Germans, Greeks, Turks and Jews. As the son of a Triestine Jewish mother, Felicita Coen, and an Italian Catholic father, Ugo Poli, who abandoned the family upon his birth, Saba also had to make an extra effort, so to speak, to embrace Italian literary culture. He not only lived in a city where, despite a majority of ethnic Italians, German in many cases remained the language of power and prestige; but his mother was dead set against his poetic vocation, and her side of the family, being Jewish in a Hapsburg city, and boasting a famous Hebrew scholar, Samuel David Luzzatto, among their close relatives, no doubt considered Italian culture merely one option among several. The major contemporary trends in Italian literature, to the adolescent Saba in Trieste, were like news from abroad, and left him relatively untouched, free to cobble together, on the basis of his highly personal readings of the classics, particularly Leopardi, his own vision of what Italian literature should be in the new century.

Of his earliest years, however, the single most determinant event, or series of events, involved his being assigned, for rough-ly the first four years of his life, to the care of his wet-nurse, a simple Slovenian Catholic woman by the name of Gioseffa ("Peppa") Sabaz (or Schobar, depending on the source), and her husband, called the "gentle butcher" in Saba's various writings. This "golden age" of early childhood, and the subsequent trauma of his separation from Peppa, when his mother came to bring him back into the family, to be brought up by her with the aid of a wealthy aunt, Zia Regina, would forever after haunt his poetry and personal life. That memory of lost happiness, and the conflicts that precipitated the separation, would become the source of one of the many splits in his identity and character. It was, perhaps, the fundamental split of his lived experience, the first and most profound sundering of a "heart divided from birth," half Jew, half Gentile, torn by "affective ambivalence" between mother and foster-mother, mother and father, self and other, solitude and society, art and life.

To such an individual, living in his distant Italo-Hapsburg town, unaffected by reigning artistic fashions and prone, by early adolescence, to breakdowns attributed to attacks of "neurasthenia," poetry became the vehicle to a possible recovery of wholeness. The world he would represent in his work would be entirely his own real world; not an ideal representation of what might be, but rather merely *that which is*, in all its simultaneous beauty and horror, darkness and light. The means by which he expressed it would be plain and blunt, generally without ornament, yet shaped to the forms of Italian verse that had inspired the young poet in his readings. By thus giving his world form, it might, in art at least, have the solidity and unity it lacked in experience, and bring the poet closer to the things he desired: love, friendship, innocence, Italy. By the very fact of being named, those things that blessed or damned his world, those fits of the heart and the objects that provoked them, might find stability and purpose; and the man himself, renamed "Saba" in homage to his beloved Peppa and the happiness he knew with her, might find a reconstituted self, as poet, in the wholeness of his self-reflecting vision.[1]

This concern for ordering, in artistic fashion, the perceptions, events and objects of one's personal, day-to-day world

[1] Many have mistakenly conjectured that Saba chose his name because it meant "bread" in Hebrew—it does not. But it is likely Saba knew the word means "grandfather" in Hebrew, given the fact that his uncle was a Hebrew scholar.

was to become the overriding force behind the poet's will to create a *canzoniere* that would present, through poetry, the sequence of his life as he had lived it, or as he wanted it to be remembered.[2] As early as 1913, when the poet was only thirty years old, he began to conceive of a broad collection that would include not all, but most of the poems of his life, especially those that represented the most salient moments of his experience as a poet and a human being. It would present them in a sort of organic sequence, with nothing superfluous, no part unrelated to the whole, and it would reflect, as an oeuvre, the very aesthetic he sought in his individual poems, which was, as he once described in a reference to Manzoni, "never to say a word that didn't correspond perfectly to his vision." This concern was to become an obsession, an ideal he felt he could never meet, but which he would nevertheless endeavor with all his might to achieve. With each new update of the *Canzoniere* (1921, '32, '43, '45, '48, '51, '57), he would naturally have new material to add, but he would also insert endless new versions of old poems, delete poems from earlier editions, give new orders to certain sequences, frequently changing his mind again when the book was in proofs. Not until later, when the Einaudi editions of the Canzoniere were published after the war, did he begin to seem at least partially satisfied with what he had done. Still, he very often criticized his inclusions and regretted his omissions, as witnessed by all the deleted poems he feels compelled to cite in his own study of the work, the *History and Chronicle of the Songbook* (1944-47). Clearly, as long as he was alive, the *Canzoniere*, that living construction of a poetic self, would remain fluid and changeable. As with life itself, only in death did the separate parts fall definitively into place, become finally unmoveable, solid as rock.

---

[2] His idea for the *Canzoniere*, according to Carlo Muscetta, was curiously based more on his reading of a contemporary Italian translation and selection of Heinrich Heine's poetry, called the *Canzoniere of Heine*, than on the famous *Canzoniere* of Petrarch or the various anthological songbooks that existed of late medieval and Renaissance Italian poetry, which were also called *canzonierei*. In the introduction to the 1961 *Antologia del Canzoniere of Saba* (Einaudi), Muscetta writes: "The Heine *Canzoniere*, organized by the translator Zendrini on the basis of organic selections from the German poet's various books, but in cyclical and chronological sequences, with prologues and epilogues, was the real model for Saba's *Canzoniere*." Saba's own claims to Heine's influence would also seem to bear this out. This said, there is no doubt, in any case, that Saba knew the very title of *Canzoniere* would evoke the great national precedent in the minds of Italian readers.

In Saba's poetry, every statement of fact is made with the utmost
solmenity. Its very utterance confers mythic significance on the
the thing uttered, granting it resonance within the personal
iconology of the Sabian corpus as a whole. Objects are conse-
crated merely by being named: places, things, people and human
events, by their very appearance in the poems, are designated as
leitmotifs. It is for this reason as well that Saba felt continually
compelled to tamper with the poems and lines that made up the
Canzoniere, for every last element was supposed to echo and mirror the life as it appeared in the art. For example, "My Foster-
Mother's House," a very early sonnet that appears as the second
poem in the definitive *Canzoniere* (though it did not come to
light until 1931, when Saba printed an edition of resuscitated and
revised juvenilia entitled *Admonition and Other Poems*), ends
with the tercet:

> To God I lifted up my peaceful soul,
> and from the house came sounds of voices
> dear to me, and the smell of supper.

These three lines, in the warmth of their emotion and tone, and
in the images evoked, establish, at the very start of his Songbook,
one locus of Saba's personal mythology, his days of innocence
and happiness at Peppa's humble home. The same images, and
the feelings associated with them, will be evoked time and again
throughout the course of his life and work. Peppa, as he states
later in "Wet-Nurse," is "the mother of joy" to whom he is
indebted for "the golden vein of happiness / running through my
song." He was to write yet another, longer poem about her
house, with the same title as the first one, included in the 1930
collection *Dying Heart*. It begins by addressing the house directly:

> O long imagined like a myth,
> or barely existing,
> where are you now, charming
> little house, portrayed in my first lines?

After having been described in physical detail in the early poem,
here the house has been so thoroughly absorbed into Saba's emotional and poetic universe as to seem "long imagined," a "myth,"

or "barely existing." Physical reality and the poet's imagination have become blurred. Now the house's primary existence lies in the meaning it bears for the poet; it was the subject of his "first lines." Long an object of the poet's desire, it has, like a memory, assumed a life of its own within the vast store of associations of the poet and the poetry. Thus when, even later, in the poem "Smoke" (from the collection *Last Things*, 1935-43), the poet, describing a wisp of smoke illuminated by a sunbeam shining through the window, says that

> it reminds me of a little house, alone
> in the fields, smoking with the evening meal

the seasoned reader, the reader familiar with the whole *Canzoniere*, knows exactly the sort of emotion the poet is trying to evoke.

This is what Saba meant when he said, writing of himself in the third person in the *History and Chronicle*, that "Saba is the least fragmentary poet of recent times." Not for him the modernist fragment, the image stripped of context, resonating in the ambiguity of its many possible interpretations. That was the domain of the Hermetic poets, that central vein of Italian modernism, which Saba never really accepted, not even when, absorbing the lessons of Ungaretti's very spare, essential verse, he arrived at the more oblique, understated poems of *Words*, *Last Things* and his later collections. For Saba life itself is fragmented enough, and poetry may even reflect this fragmentation so long as it does not compromise what he believed to be its essential task: to be true to its inspiration. And since his own inspiration arose from the life around him, from his desperate need to give order and meaning to that life, he would strike the same chords again and again, providing ultimately a choral resonance to the individual moments represented in his oeuvre. In his 1911 essay on poetics, "The Remaining Task of Poets" (published only posthumously), Saba criticizes the modern obsession with originality at all costs:

> I even think that the fear of repeating oneself is harm-
> ful. When a feeling is innate, and the need for expres-
> sion is innate, it is only natural that, so long as a man
> cannot come out of himself, this feeling and expression
> should be repeated, with the obsessiveness of someone
> who feels something that no words or sounds or any

external means can ever render to perfection. Hence the dissatisfaction one feels after every work, and the hope that one will say it better next time . . . . And if the inspiration is sincere, and thus is subject to the power of the specific moment in which it is born, it will always have, no matter how many times it is repeated, something that distinguishes it.

The contents of the "Juvenilia and Early Works" in the definitive *Canzoniere* confirm just how seriously Saba took such statements as the above, and to what degree he sought to keep true to his inspiration. In that final, much-revised representation of the poet as a youth, we find poems that cover nearly all the thematics that will concern him over the course of his career: transience ("Admonition"); lost happiness and innocence ("My Foster-Mother's House"); his love and ambivalence toward his mother ("Spring Sonnet," "To Mama"); his separateness from others ("Glauco"); his wish to join with others ("Dream of a Conscript"); his passion for his wife ("To Lina"); the city of Trieste ("From a Hilltop").[3] At no time in his career, not even during the more "abstract" phase of the *Prelude and Fugues*, will he stray from these central concerns and the personal, direct voice giving them expression. Of course, since Saba's is a poetry pre-eminently dictated by circumstance, there will be no lack of new subjects and interests to write about as he journeys through life. Yet the core will remain the same, the work will remain as distinct, as self-defined, as the man who wrote it.

*

Unlike so many of his contemporaries, Saba was not troubled, in his writing, by the modern "crisis of representation." He is primarily a poet of statement who writes with the confidence to assert whatever he wishes and a will to name things as they are. There is no *glissement* here, no shadow of doubt, between signifier and signified. He is perfectly content to open a poem with a line such as "It is night, raging winter," and to assume that the simple words themselves, in their very existence as poetry, will evoke the circumstances and emotions from which they arose. The Mallarmean-Symbolist poetics of suggestion

[3] Because of obvious limitations of space and time, not all of these poems are included in this selection.

and indirectness, which had filtered into Italian poetry through D'Annunzio and Pascoli before ultimately being distilled into a more indigenous vein by Ungaretti and Montale, never affected him at all. As he wrote of himself around 1944, under the guise of Giuseppe Carimandrei, in the *History and Chronicle*,

> Saba has always felt that, wherever heartfelt necessity presents itself, anything can be said, in verse as in prose; that to have limited poetry to the expression of a few "moments" (however luminous) was one of the errors born of the mistrust and weariness that were in the air at the time; and that every extreme of "refinement" leads—in art as in life—to an extreme of impoverishment.

Also unlike his contemporaries, Saba had no gripe whatsoever with the traditional forms and themes of Italian poetry, or with the classical hendecasyllabic line and its various natural breakdowns into shorter verse lines. While he did, on occasion, write free verse, especially later in his career, it quite often contains echoes and even fragments of the hendecasyllable, a highly variable, elastic line to begin with. His *Canzoniere*, moreover, counts endless sonnets, canzoni, canzonettas, ballades and so forth (the last three being highly variable forms in themselves), along with the open forms he loved so skilfully to create using traditional verse lines and variable or fixed rhymes. Gianfranco Contini, the eminent critic and scholar of Italian poetry from its origins to the modern age, once wrote that "presiding over the birth of [Saba's] verse, there is always I know not what act of homage to traditional elements, any and all." The timeless premises of lyric, especially the Italian lyric, thrive in Saba: love first and foremost, the will to song, the impulses of desire, the inner movements of the poet's heart—all are as prominent in the *Canzoniere* as in the Italian poetry of any age. If art must be mimetic in "classical" fashion, as Saba felt that it must, then the lyric, as in Cavalcanti, Petrarch or Leopardi, can only imitate the poet's life.

It is, if anything, in the life, and in the language used to represent the life, that the poetry strikes us, as it did his contemporaries, as radically "modern." For while Saba so lovingly clung to the forms of the Italian tradition, he was as determined as his avant-garde contemporaries were to "wring the neck of eloquence" (Montale), that is, to give poetry a language more proper to the modern experience than the highly rhetorical, "aulic" language that had come down through the centuries from the great origins of Italian poetry and eventually had become so academic and baroque as to be obscure and unwieldy. This project of renovation had, of course, been in progress to one degree or another in Italy since the latter 19th century, but at no time previous did it acquire so immediate a sense of urgency as in the first two decades of the twentieth century. And it was in this very period that Saba quite instinctively found his own personal, unrhetorical register, even as the *crepuscolari*, the Futurists, and the poets of *La Voce* (Dino Campana, Camillo Sbarbaro et al) were seeking far different ways to renew Italian poetry.

He found it in the simple premise of thrusting his own life and experiences, raw and concise, directly into verse. A tercet from a sonnet in the cycle entitled "While Marching," written during Saba's tour of military service in 1908, well illustrates this point.

> Around me the faces are sweaty and ugly.
> I look at my companion, his tongue hanging
> half-out, as on a slaughtered steer.

The simplicity of statement, the sharply drawn images, the immediacy of the action (the poem is "occurring" during the marching drill), the subdued tone and quiet confidence, all of it hewing closely to the demands of traditional form (the original is rhymed and metered), signalled something new. They pointed to the possibility that ancient form might indeed accomodate modern experience. As always with Saba, however, it would require time and an accumulation of impressions for this novelty to become more strikingly apparent; it might not be immediately evident to a reader familiar with only one or two poems. He certainly was not averse to taking "poetic license" and resorting to old-fashioned devices such as anastrophe, ellipsis and archaisms, when the form and verse line seemed to demand it, or when he thought it might enhance the desired effect. Moreover, his "quiet" tone might even be mistaken, at times, for the "crepuscular" manner, a misunderstanding that indeed plagued Saba for the early part of his career. Not, perhaps, until the full range of Saba's preoccupations had emerged, and the power with which he experienced his personal conflicts and passions had found its full expression in verse, would the originality of his vision and style begin to be appreciated by his contemporaries.

This need to be read comprehensively, combined with some of the other factors discussed above—above all his formal choices and his living in Trieste—led to Saba's famous literary isolation, from which he would not emerge, at least professionally, until after World War II. (One might say that he never emerged from it personally.) Still, despite all the poet's bitter complaints in this regard, especially in the *History and Chronicle* and in his letters, he became, perhaps somewhat unbeknownst to himself, quite well respected by other poets and critics by the time he had reached his late 30s. Even at the start of his career, the novelty and moral power of his work was evident enough to the editors of the *Voce* group to warrant their publishing -- despite the fact that, in his own words, "among them I was of another species"— his first two volumes (in 1911 and 1912) under their imprint, even though he, like so many, had to pay the costs of publication. If this association with the Florentine group ended badly for the poet—in an utter lack of critical or commercial response to those two volumes—it probably was not due to any malice such as he attributed (in the *History and Chronicle*) to the editor-poet Giovanni Papini and his associates, but rather to professional ineptitude on the part of their group in general.[4]

However that may be, if Saba was able to assert the importance of his "difference" in a literary milieu hostile, at least formalistically, to the means he had chosen to employ in his verse, it was, to repeat, because he had succeeded in fitting radically novel subject matter and style into old clothing. "No one scorned the old themes and analogies less than he," writes Saba of himself. True as this may be, it was nevertheless in the way he made his new subject matter fit the old themes and forms that he made his lasting mark on Italian poetry. For example, while love has been the dominant theme of the Italian lyric since its medieval beginnings, never has there been a poem remotely like his justly famous "To My Wife," which in its sincerity of passion, its fabular exemplarity, its pure, earthly realism and humble tone, stands quite apart from traditional Italian love poems, which have almost always tended metaphysically to idealize the beloved.

---

[4] Indeed, in another literary misadventure, not without historic consequences, Papini's associate, poet-painter Ardengo Soffici, lost, in 1914, the only existing manuscript of Dino Campana's now famous *Canti orfici*, which the already unstable Campana then had to reconstitute entirely from memory. He wrote very little thereafter, spending much of the remainder of his short life in and out of asylums.

It opens:

> You are like
> a young white hen,
> with feathers ruffled
> in the wind, who bends her neck
> to drink and scratch the ground
> yet walks with your same slow
> and queenly step,
> proud and puffed-up
> as she struts onto the grass.

This odd, ecstatic realism was utterly new. The elevation of a traditionally comic (and thus "low") animal to the sublime heights of amorous devotion not by means of hyperbole, but by sheer virtue of precise description and the poet's emotional sincerity, had no precedent. Similarly, the cycle of poems entitled "New Lines to Lina," in Trieste and a Woman (1910-12), precipitated by a conjugal crisis the specifics of which Saba never divulged, presents a highly personal ferocity and tenderness, a starkly frank ambivalence the likes of which had never been seen before in Italian poetry. The emotional charge of the poet's desperate, exasperated cries appears on the page highly mediated by the form yet no less immediate and sincere for being wrought into song:

> A woman, a petty little thing,
> my God! A wretched thing indeed.
> And then one like her, ever more concealed
> inside herself, who every morning seems
> to take up less room in the world,
> to give a life its due in sorrow.

Here, as always in Saba, there is a tension between the specificity of the feeling and the spareness of the details presented. Enough particulars are given to paint a realistic picture, yet the scene is rendered in a voice so authentic it leaves many things out, as we often do in speech, and thus manages at once to create an effect of utter personalism and general, universal circumstance. This tension between form and content, between subjectivity and objectivity, is reflected on many different levels in Saba's verse, including, quite notably, the purely linguistic and formal level, where the conflict between an absolute naturalness of speech and the syntactical irregularities permitted in Italian verse—sometimes necessitated by the rigor of its metrics—resolves, in his finest moments, in an utter transparency of form, which shines all the more for its contrast with those passages where the language strains to the demands of economy. The visible craft, like the personal experience, is the precondition for the invisible, universal poetry that results.

In this sort of poetry, it is only natural, perhaps, that the relationship, and tension, between the poet's acute subjectivity and the objects of his perceptions and desire should represent per se a constant thematics. In his work as in his life, Saba was forever struggling at once to affirm his extreme individuality and to be part of the world around him. Ungaretti called Saba "the poet of himself," yet for Saba the assertion of this self always entails meeting the world halfway. The counterpoint, in Saba's poetry, between self and other, between the inner life and the outside world, between the ego and society, is forever renewing itself, constantly donning new guises and registers of expression. Saba's Trieste, for example, the city of his isolation and identity, functions as his Leopardian *ermo colle*, the "lonely hill" from which, with all its limitations, the poet may experience the infinite universe; it is from the solitude of his antiquarian bookshop in Trieste, a "living showcase of the dead," that, in sonnet 15 of *Autobiography*, he writes:

> and all that lay beyond his time and space
> his art portrayed more beautifully
> to him, his song made sweeter still.

But Trieste also serves, in all its isolation and "difference," as the key to his becoming, in all his idiosyncrasy, the poet of Italy. Saba had always felt that as a Triestine, he had a fresh eye on the old forms and figures of the Italian tradition, and could, so to speak, give them back to Italy renewed. So strong is this feeling that, even from the depths of his despair, while hiding from the Germans in Florence in 1944, he writes of Trieste, "I married her to Italy with song," reasserting his (and the city's) dream of belonging, even in the most hostile circumstances.[5]

All of Saba's passions and infatuations—his love for Lina

---

[5] His hope may well have been nourished by the protection and care he received from Italians sheltering him from the Nazis and Italian fascists who saught to deport him with other Italian Jews. (See the *History and Chronicle*, pp.   ).

and Peppa, his flirtations with young women and men, his wish to be "only a man / among men"—express this *outward* movement of his poetic impulse and complement his *inward* impulse to plumb the depths of his own soul. For Saba it is never enough to know that his vocation, his character, and the circumstances of his birth have set him apart from others. He wants forever to be part of things, to belong to the community of mankind. Indeed, perhaps it is because he is so different, because he is a poet prone to nervous breakdowns, because he is from a broken home, because he is a Jew from Trieste, that he wants so desperately to be Italian, to have a "normal" life selling antique books, to be

> . . . outside
> of myself, to live the life
> of everyone,
> to be like every
> everyday
> man.
>
> ("The Town")

Yet never is he willing to relinquish the things that make him different, the innate sorrow, the "wound of birth" that he is nevertheless trying forever to heal. He would, he must, have it both ways. The result is the same whether the object of his desire is the human community or his wife Lina. Of Lina he says in "The Wife," a poem from *Trieste and a Woman,*

> How can my angel ever understand
> that there is nothing in the world
> I wouldn't share with her but this,
> this speechless pain; and that my sufferings
> are mine, they belong only to my soul.
> I will not give them up for wife or daughter,
> or dole them out in equal parts to loved ones.

Indeed, in his "heart divided from birth," the two things—the generous, outward reaching man and the tortured, self-regarding solipsist—must coexist if Saba is to exist at all. This becomes particularly clear in "The Town," the very poem in which he perhaps most thoroughly and clearly expressed his long-existing yearning to be part of the world. For no sooner has the poet expressed his wish to be like the common man,

> . . . to say
> and do things

that are,
like bread and wine,
like women and children,
beloved
of all . . .

than he realizes that the dilemma lies in the very wish:

But still, alas!
I left a little corner for my yearning, a chink
of blue sky
from which I might behold myself
and taste the joy
of no longer being myself
but only a man
among men.

In these lines, as in the poetry as a whole, both impulses exist at once, and hence the poet feels regret. The key to the problem, and to the twofold essence of Saba the man and poet, lies in the line: *"from which I might behold myself."* For in the very act of wishing to join with humanity he is, like it or not, still looking on himself, acknowledging a pain that we know he would never relinquish.

Yet for all the suffering it caused him, or indeed because of it, Saba was able to plumb this sundering of self—so deep in his personal constitution yet so universal in its symbolic import — to rich and varied poetic effect. It is the invisible fault line running through the sonnet sequence of *Autobiography*, in which utterly personal events crystallize into limpid but dense poem-objects; and it is also what allows him, so to speak, to step outside of himself and write the sonnet cycle of *Prisoners*, each of which represents a character type from the human family but speaks in the first person, as if each representing one aspect of Saba's psyche as well. For Saba's struggle with the world indeed parallels the struggles constantly being waged among the different sides of himself: Saba is at once the son of his mother, whose outlook is fraught with Biblical pessimism and fatalism, and of his father, the lighthearted but irresponsible drifter, the so-called "murderer" (as he was known to the poet "for the twenty years until I met him") who was "light and cheerful, while my mother / bore the weight of all life's burdens"; Saba is both the wise realist for whom "some little thing sufficed, / from time to time," but also the obsessive-compulsive still looking for his lost "good thought" in "the blind mazes of hell"; he is at once the passionate husband of Lina, the assiduous suitor of various young women, and the homosexual hinted at repeatedly throughout the *Canzoniere*, yet not given full expression until the novel *Ernesto*, written late in life and published posthumously; he is at once the young soldier who laments having to witness things "too Jewish, too fat or too lean," and the young poet who cherishes the Jewish cemetery in Trieste

> whenever I think of my forebears lying there
> after lifetimes of suffering and trade,
> all of like mind and appearance.

("Three Streets")

And if the dark side, in reality, seems often to get the better of the "golden vein of happiness" in Saba's poetry, if the tortured egotist seems perhaps to win out over the serene altruist, the very act of casting the conflict into verse creates an overriding luminosity in which may lie some hope of resolution or transcendence:

> My road is sad but brightened by the sun;
> and everything on it, even shadow, is in light.

("To My Soul")

Nowhere, perhaps, does this tension strike so pure and effective a balance as in the poems of the *Prelude and Fugues* (1928-29). Whereas previously Saba had moved back and forth between emotional and spiritual extremes from poem to poem, in the Fugues he gives each pole of each dichotomy a voice of its own, and lets them speak to one another within one same poem: pessimism echoes optimism, love echoes hate, introversion echoes extroversion, and so on, creating a counterpoint in which at times the voices even come to overlap and eventually exchange roles (as in the Third Fugue). Each voice may represent a single figure (such as optimism) or a compendium of interrelated characteristics (such as introspection, jealous love and spirituality). The overall effect of their dialogue is musical, yet the values given each sung "note" are clearly charged with semantic and emotional meaning, resulting in a highly distilled poetry of familiar, contrasting themes harmoniously coexisting in their simultaneous resonance. In the most complex of these compositions, the Sixth Fugue, the so-called "Canto in Three Voices" (all the other Fugues have only two voices), the "third voice" stands as it were outside, or above the other two, embodying at once their resolution and the object of their desire: muse, nymph, angel, poetry. In their purely aesthetic serenity, the *Fugues* represent Saba's most limpid resolution of the various conflicts of his soul.

Art, however, may resolve conflicts in art, but it may not always do so in life. Shortly after composing the *Fugues*, Saba entered a period of psychoanalysis after suffering, in 1929, yet another of his many "nervous crises." The renewed exploration of his troubled past resulted in the cycle of poems entitled "Little Berto" (1929-31), in which the poet reverts to the more strictly autobiographical mode. Here Saba again revisits, perhaps as never before, the places and events of his early childhood, particularly his separation from Peppa; he also interrogates himself as a child, and even goes to visit the present-day Peppa, whom he hasn't seen in a long time. Curiously, in the *History and Chronicle*, Saba is rather critical of these poems, claiming they are "excessive," and that "the names of Zia Stellina, Elvira and Peppa had an evocative power [to him] that they could never have had for the reader." On a strictly personal level he may be right in saying this; on a poetic level he is greatly underestimating himself. In these poems he is, as always, returning to his origins to heal "the wound of birth." He is also obeying his same rule of *consecration through naming;* the only difference here is that he utters his statements presuming (sometimes) a familiarity with the subject, something which he may have thought weighted them down with the burden of specific reference, especially after the self-sufficient, ethereal purity of the *Fugues*.

The psychoanalytic confrontation with the self, however, was soon to bear its fruit in other ways. As he himself expressed in the *History and Chronicle*, psychoanalysis ultimately brought about a "clarification" in the poetry. This becomes immediately evident in in the poems of the 1933-34 collection *Words*, which follow hard upon the heels of *Little Berto* but mark a turning point in his approach to writing. The language becomes more spare, generally (but not always) less metrically strict, less narrative in exposition, more given to highlighting the specific weight of individual words. It shows, to a degree, an appreciation (somewhat late, by his own admission) of the lessons of Giuseppe Ungaretti, for whom the act of composition was a process of gradual refinement and reduction to the bare, luminous essentials. But Saba's new mode, which would continue in the next collection, *Last Things* (1933-43), and remain the dominant one in his verse for the remainder of his life, in no wise consitituted a compromise to the trends of the time, which Saba had always fiercely resisted. It is the product of a maturation, a new self-assuredness of composition, in which the poet feels free to express himself in simpler gestures. He has merely condensed his long-established approach to writing.[6] The typical spareness of detail has been reduced to the quintessential. The new poems remain entirely his own, and continue to treat the problems and thematics of his entire oeuvre. With the new "clarification," in fact, the dialectic between subject and object, between the poet and the world, finds novel expression as objects take on greater importance in themselves, as subjects of poetry.

> Greens, fruit, colors of the bright
> season. A few baskets, to thirsty eyes,
> reveal sweet, raw pulp.

> ("Greengrocer")

The poet has, so to speak, managed to find himself in things. They are still subject to the lyric gaze, but sometimes, as here, that gaze manages to be almost invisible. Many, still, are the poems centered entirely in the poet's subjective experience, yet with the greater distance from the world outside has come a paradoxical reconciliation of sorts. There is a quiet wisdom to these later works, a new ability to glean the moral lessons of experience, however bitter they might be.

> There, now you know our place is not
> among the blessed; and that life,
> like avid eyes, is full
> of hidden tears.

> ("There, Now You Know")

[6] This process is analyzed in detail in a series of lectures given at the University of Rome in 1958-59 by Giacomo Debenedetti, in which he presents an illuminating treatment of the later Saba's relationship to Hermeticism. These lectures have been reprinted, in part, in *Poesia Italiana del Novecento*, Garzanti, Milan, 1980).

Even with World War II looming on the horizon, and with the passage of the Fascist "Racial Laws" in 1938, which prohibited Jews and those of "mixed race" from publishing and holding public jobs, Saba managed to preserve the relative serenity of his new approach.[7] It was only with the fall of the Mussolini government in 1943 and the subsequent German occupation of the peninsula—when Saba's bookshop was sequestered by Nazi authorities and he had to go into hiding to avoid being deported—that he briefly returned to his former, more discursive mode of writing, in a desperate search for answers to the "age-old useless questions." This moment was not to last, however, and all of his postwar collections of poetry resume the mature style, while showing as well an increased tendency to rewrite classical myths, to revive the fabular mode, once an old favorite, and to use animals (especially birds) as emblematic subjects.

The national fame Saba found after the War, and the growing commitment he felt to expressing his life in prose, seem not to have affected the later poetry, except perhaps in providing an outlet to the poet's perennial narrative urge, which allowed the poems to remain succinct and lyrically pure. Saba by now had, in his own words, "less things to narrate (at least in verse), and more things to sing about." Restored at last (although at first with some reluctance) to his old lair at the back of his bookshop in Trieste, he was free again to find his moments of light in the dark matter of existence, despite his own and his wife's failing health. But Saba had never really feared death, had almost welcomed it at times "as the resolution of all" and "sole comfort of the vanquished," and in these final years he continued determinedly down his same, now much-worn path, still finding poetry in life's many, varied moments, still trying to find the right combination to the poems of his *Canzoniere*, still wishing, despite his greater celebrity, that his countrymen would understand him as he thought he understood himself. No matter. As death resolves the life, poetry defies the death: "Ancient, / it shall, like oak, withstand decay."

---

[7] Actually Saba, like many Italian Jews of relative importance, managed in part to get around these restrictions. He refrained from publishing any books, but was able to publish poems ina variety of magazines. When the Germans finally invaded, however, the situation became far more dangerous.

By the time Umberto Saba died in 1957, at the age of 74, many of the aesthetic and ideological distinctions that had so stridently served to define the different styles of art and poetry of the first half of the century had begun to fall away, and much of the work produced over those fifty years could be reassessed with eyes less troubled, and perhaps less dazzled, than before. Even the monolith of Hermeticism had begun to crumble as a concept, to the point where the term had come to mean little more to general readers than a certain impenetrability they associated with "modern" poetry. Ungaretti himself, long considered the "grandfather" of Hermeticism (Montale's hermeticism had always been somewhat in question), had long looked on the term with more than a little skepticism.[8] By 1962, in fact, critic Luciano Anceschi, in his important study, *Poetiche del Novecento in Italia*, individuated a new category that both distinguished Ungaretti and Montale from the lesser modernist figures who shared their same concern with reconciling experiment and tradition, and grouped the two great poets with Umberto Saba, with whom they shared the distinction, despite their vast individual differences, of having brought a strongly lyric poetry back into the center of Italian literary culture. And Anceschi termed his triumvirate, quite appropriately, the "new lyric poets," consciously linking them, by virtue of their reassertion of the lyric "I" in the face of the century's attempts to squash the individual, to the great lyric tradition of the Italian past. In the cases of Ungaretti and Montale, this "return to tradition" was a conscious choice made more or less in mid-career; in Saba's case, it was something that had been there from the start, the very ground, so to speak, from which his verse sprung.

In yet another camp, the vast new school of "Neo-Realism" that arose from the rubble of the war to dominate the Italian cultural landscape of the late '40s and '50s, also looked to Saba as a "precursor," seeing in his celebration of the simple human event,

[8] Acutally the term more properly applies to teh generation that followed these poets, which includes such major figures as Salvatore Quasimodo, Mario Luzi and Vittorio Sereni. Nevertheless the origins of the current—so-called, among other reasons becasue of its strongly "analogical" approach to poetic language—can be traced back to the *Voce* group adn beyond, to late 19th-century French poetry (cf., among others, L. Anceschi, *Poetiche del novecento in Italia*).

his love of the "common man" and his realistic rendering of life, a foreshadowing of their own unembellished, often brutal presentations of life in film, fiction, photography, painting and poetry. The irony here is that, for all the aesthetic simplicity of their art, the Neo-Realists, too, were highly theoretical and ideological in their intellectual self-justifications and never shy about anathematizing work that to them might seem too "decadent," "rhetorical" (read D'Annunzian and hence "proto-Fascist") or "traditional." Even more ironic, perhaps, is that amidst all these aesthetic and ideological shifts, Saba, by merely being himself, was finally vindicated. All he had ever really said, in a "theoretical" vein—and he had said it in 1911, in the unpublished essay "The Remaining Task of Poets"—was that the poet should make "honest" poetry. That is, that the poet should never exceed the authentic self; should never force inspiration; should never overreach for originality; should not be afraid to repeat himself or what others have said; should be a seeker of truth, not success; and should be a moral figure unto his fellow humans, not a professional among professionals. And all he had ever done was to try as much as possible to remain true to these tenets in practice.

As Guido Piovene wrote, in article entitled "The Poetry of Love's Joys and Sorrows,"

> The lesson that Saba teaches . . . is one of consistency. This poet may have perfected himself as much as you like; still, he has remained, from his beginnings to this day, clearly, inexorably, and with a kind of gentle firmness, true to himself. Saba's strength—his poetry's strength, that is—lies in never having yielded to any of the different poetics with which many of his contemporaries, in our troubled Europe, have inoculated themseves with the same indiscriminate violence with which modern medicine has arrogantly inoculated the population with their sera. This, perhaps, is his secret, the thing that makes him, and has always made him, at once so ancient and so new. A miracle—inherent in his nature, and in no way provoked by him—has happened to Saba: that is, while today people are seeking a "cure" with polemical fury and impatiently refashioning a form and content for poetry, Saba can peacefully stand pat. [9]

[9] Quoted in the *History and Chronicle of the Songbook*, The Sheep Meadow Press, Riverdale-on-Hudson, NY, 1998, p.   )

And he could also "stand pat" because, without his having tried, he had lived an emblematically "modern" life, and had turned that life into art. In a certain sense, the very same middle-class drama of the 19th-century novel of England and France, so rarely given voice in 19th-century Italy, can be said to find its lyric expression in Saba, in the tranformed context of the thrilling and violent 20th century, when Italy, too, joined the ranks of the industrial powers, with all the advantages, brutality and alienation that membership brought with it. Saba is the *homme moyen sensuel* of 20th-century poetry, living archetypally as poet, an alien like everyone one else, wanting to be "just like every / everyday man." The motivation—and the necessary limitation—of his verse is the fact of being human. In that humanity and its limitation lie a natural sublimity and modernity that need not be forced to become poetry.

For Saba's modernism is ultimately what one might term the "other" modernism, the modernism not of form but of subject, of experience, a modernism of firm and solid image and diction beyond the fireworks and confusion of the polemics and schools: it is the modernism of the sober Camus, the colloquial Frost, the Williams of the red wheelbarrow and the plums in the refrigerator. Perhaps above all it is the modernism of the artist who must at all costs define his own terms and stake out his own turf in the cultural landscape. It may seem curious to readers of the *History and Chronicle* that Saba should feel so compelled, in that book, to assert his own importance when so many others had already done so. Yet the need he feels goes hand in hand with that which drove him so obsessively to revise his *Canzoniere*. In the modern age, where the cultural ground we walk on shifts and drops like quicksand, no outside endorsement, however strong and sincere, can be sufficient to an artist like Saba. The artist must shape the very frame in which his painting is to hang. And this *epistemological* effort brings Saba round full circle to the very avant-gardes he so disdained. For his art, like theirs, must create its own institution, having arisen from an imperative of change.

Thus it is hardly surprising that even now, with the repeated revival of avantgardism in Italy over the last three decades, Saba's place among the giants of the Italian century remains unchallenged. He sits secure, *tel qu'en lui-même enfin l'éternité le change*, still gazing at the world "with new eyes in the ancient evening." In Italy Saba is by now a household name, and much beloved of the common reader, no doubt because of the straightforwardness and clarity of his *Canzoniere*.[10] Still there is a relative lack of scholarship on his work, even in Italian, compared to that which exists on the poetry of Ungaretti and Montale. This may be in part due to the clarity and openness of the work, since scholars seem more drawn by nature to things that demand explanation (though Saba's work is never so simple as it seems). But there is still no critical Italian edition of the complete poems, no doubt because the endless variants and combinations that Saba produced of his poems over the years would require several thousand-page tomes to cover them all. And while the Mondadori "Meridiani" edition of *Tutte le Poesie* is a highly useful compendium, with extensive, seperate chronologies of the life and work, it certainly does not contain "all the poems," omitting some of the minor work which the poet excluded even from his *Canzoniere apocrifo* (included in Mondadori edition), but which could easily be tracked down in extant "slim volumes" and manuscripts.

And of course there is very little scholarship on Saba in English. In fact, most educated readers hardly know him beyond the customarily anthologized pieces. It is my hope that this book will have made some small contribution toward improving that situation.

---

[10] Saba had, in fact, once considered entitling the *Canzoniere* "*Chiarezza*" ("Clarity").

Note to the Text

The challenge of rendering, in another language, the color, tone and effects of a master formalist such as Umberto Saba, is one of the most daunting a literary translator ever has to face. Saba's verse, morever, has oddities quite peculiar to him. He shuns, for example, the "grand manner" of the past and some of his older contemporaries, yet jealously reserves the right to use any of its rhetorical expedients when necessary, even when writing free verse. His language, while strikingly modern and unaffected, nevertheless displays a purity of diction that one could only call "classical," so much so that when the poet used to read his compositions aloud, he would shed the strong Triestine intonations of his regular speech and assume a pure, more Tuscan pronunciation. I have tried as much as possible to reproduce these sorts of peculiarities—the coexistence of colloquial diction and *il fare antico*, of limpidity and occasional, dense knots of language, of intense personalism and objective concreteness—while bearing in mind the demands of our American idiom and the options of the great English tradition out of which it has grown. Sometimes, to achieve these ends, I have had to forego some of the formal aspects of the original, usually the rhyme; at other times I was more fortunate. Thus some sonnets, for example, are rhymed, while others are not. The reader will, I hope, forgive this apparent inconsistency; it was dictated by the necessities of fidelity and taste, which naturally varied from poem to poem. Giacomo Debenedetti wrote that Saba serves two masters: music and the concrete word. I have tried, within the limits faced by all translators, to do the same.

All of the poems here presented are in the same, chronological order in which they appear in Saba's final *Canzoniere*, with the exception of the poem "To My Soul," which the publisher and I have chosen as a kind of frontispiece to this selection. The Italian texts of the poems are from *Tutte le poesie*, Mondadori, 1994, and the 1965 Einaudi *Canzoniere*. In making my selection, I relied above all on those two editions and on three editions of selected poems: *Antologia del Canzoniere*, Carlo Muscetta ed., Einaudi, 1963; *Poesie scelte*, Giovanni Giudici ed., Mondadori, 1976; and *Il Canzoniere*, Folco Portinari ed., Einaudi 1976. My choices, however, were mostly determined by my own judgment. The *Canzoniere* is a vast, sprawling compendium of a lifetime of work (638 pages, not including the *Canzoniere apocrifo*, which counts some 330 more pages); the poems often echo one another in a way that makes isolating individual pieces for a selection such as this a difficult task. In general I have tried to choose poems that most successfully showcase Saba's talents and best represent the different phases of his poetic career, within the limits imposed by time and feasibility. The best poems don't always work in English, or in my English at least. Saba, in the words of critic Franco Rella, was "forever coming back to the words we already have." I hope, here, to have let Saba speak in the words we already have.

For the initial idea of translating Saba, I am deeply indebted to the publisher, editor and poet Stanley Moss, who has long felt the need for a substantial selection of Saba in English translation, and who provided sensitive, insightful editorial suggestions on these versions at every step of the process. Special thanks to professor A Mandelbaum for his professional support and forr his putting me in touch with Stanley Moss and the Sheep Meadow Press. And for his invaluable help in clarifying some of the more difficult passages in the poems I would like to thank my friend Prof. Manfredi Piccolomini of Lehman College, who has graciously been answering my questions for the last two years. For their patient support and assistance, both technical and emotional, many thanks also go to my late father, Dr. Corrado Sartarelli; my mother, Anna Lazotti-Deutsch; my wife, Sophie Hawkes; my friend Thomas Epstein; and my former colleague Prof. Maria Assunta Nicoletti of Bard College. Without them it would have been a much longer road.

VOLUME I

1900-1920

All'anima mia

Dell'inesausta tua miseria godi.
Tanto ti valga, anima mia, sapere;
sì che il tuo male, null'altro, ti giovi.

O forse avventurato è chi s'inganna?
né a se stesso scoprirsi ha in suo potere,
né mai la sua sentenza lo condanna?

Magnanima sei pure, anima nostra;
ma per quali non tuoi casi t'esalti,
sì che un bacio mentito indi ti prostra.

A me la mia miseria è un chiaro giorno
d'estate, quand'ogni aspetto dagli alti
luoghi discopro in ogni suo contorno.

Nulla m'è occulto; tutto è sì vicino
dove l'occhio o il pensiero mi conduce.
Triste ma soleggiato è il mio cammino;

e tutto in esso, fino l'ombra, è in luce.

(1912)

To My Soul

You delight in your unending misery.
Such, my soul, should be the worth of knowledge,
that your suffering alone should do you good.

Or is the self-deceived the lucky one?
he who cannot ever know himself
or the sentence of his condemnation?

Still, my soul, you are magnanimous;
yet how you thrill to phantom opportunities,
and so are brought down by a faithless kiss.

To me my misery is a bright summer
day, where from high up I can make out
every facet, every detail of the world below.

Nothing is obscure to me; it's all right there,
wherever my eye or my mind leads me.
My road is sad but brightened by the sun;

and everything on it, even shadow, is in light.

(1912)

from

POESIE DELL ADOLESCENZA E GIOVANILI

JUVENILIA AND EARLY WORKS

(1900-1907)

La casa della mia nutrice

La casa della mia nutrice posa
tacita in faccia alla Cappella antica,
ed al basso riguarda, e par pensosa,
da una collina alle caprette amica.

La città dove nacqui popolosa
scopri da lei per la finestra aprica;
anche hai la vista de mar dililettosa
e di campagne grate alla fatica.

Qui—mi sovviene—nell'eta primiera,
del vecchio camposanto fra le croci,
giocavo ignaro sul far della sera.

A Dio innalzavo l'anima serena;
e dalla casa un suon di care voci
mi giungeva, e l'odore della cena.

My Foster Mother's House

My foster mother's house stands silent
opposite the ancient Chapel, looking down,
as if in thought, from a hillside
friendly to the herds of goats.

From its sunny window you can take in
at a glance the crowded city of my birth;
you also have delightful views of the sea
and the fields alive with human labor.

Here, I remember, I used to play
in early boyhood, oblivious, as evening
fell, among old crosses in the graveyard.

To God I lifted up my peaceful soul,
and from the house came sounds of voices
dear to me, and the smell of supper.

Sonetto di Primavera

Città paesi e culmini lontani
sorridon lieti al sol di primavera.
Torna serena la natia riviera.
Sono pieni di canti il mare e i piani.

Io solo qui di desideri vani
t'esalto, mia inesperta anima altera;
poi stanco mi riduco in sulla sera
alla mia stanza, e incerto del domani.

Là seggo sovra il bianco letticciolo,
e ripenso a un'età già tramontata,
a un amor che mi strugge, all'avvenire.

E se nell'ombra odo la voce amata
di mia madre appressarsi e poi morire,
spesso col pianto vo addolcendo il duolo.

Spring Sonnet

Cities and towns and faraway hills
gleam with joy in the springtime sun.
My native shore again grows still
and sea and fields resound with song.

Here, alone, with vain yearnings I excite
you, my proud and still unseasoned soul.
Then weary to my room I go as night
begins to fall, uncertain of tomorrow.

There I sit down on the white bedcovers
and think of a time gone by with speed,
a love that consumes me, my future years.

And if in the dark I hear my mother's
precious voice draw near and then recede,
I often sweeten my sorrow with tears.

Glauco

Glauco, un fanciullo dalla chioma bionda,
dal bel vestito di marinaretto,
e dall'occhio sereno, con gioconda
voce mi disse, nel natio dialetto:

Umberto, ma perché senza un diletto
tu consumi la vita, e par nasconda
un dolore o un mistero ogni tuo detto?
Perché non vieni con me sulla sponda

del mare, che in sue azzurre onde c'invita?
Qual è il pensiero che non dici, ascoso,
e che da noi, così a un tratto, t'invola?

Tu non sai come sia dolce la vita
agli amici che fuggi, e come vola
a me il mio tempo, allegro e immaginoso.

Glauco

Glauco, a boy with a blond head of hair
and clear blue eyes, dressed in a handsome
little sailor's suit, asked me in a cheerful
voice, speaking in his native dialect:

Umberto, why do you go through your life
without a single pleasure, and seem to
hide some pain or mystery in everything
you say? Why don't you come with me and we'll

go to the sea and swim in its blue waves?
What trouble can't you talk about, what
is it calls you from us without warning?

You have no idea how sweet life can be
to the friends you flee, and how the time
flies by for me, so fanciful and light.

from

VERSI MILITARI

MILITARY POEMS

(1908)

Bersaglio

Del mare sulle iridescenti arene,
dove in trincee si ammucchiano, mi getto;
e con una repressa ansia il grilletto
premo. Va la terribile frustata

e una sagoma cade. Immaginata
non ho in essa una piùbella che buona,
non una testa che porti corona,
non il nemico che piùmai non viene.

Se qui l'occhio non falla e il colpo è certo,
egli è che nel bersaglio ognor figuro
l'orrore che i miei occhi hanno sofferto.

Tutto che di deforme hanno veduto,
di troppo ebraico, di troppo panciuto,
di troppo lamentosamente impuro.

Target

On the seashore's iridescent sands, where
soldiers fill the trenches, I fall to the ground
with quiet dread and curl my finger round
the trigger. The crack rends the air

and a silhouette falls. But in that form
I've never imagined a woman more
beautiful than good, a head with a crown, or
some never-present foe in uniform.

If my eye is true, and my aim is sure,
it's that in the target I always picture
the horrors my eyes have had to endure:

all of the unsightly things they've seen,
things too Jewish, too fat or too lean,
things all too lamentably impure.

Dopo il silenzio

Mentre il compagngo lamentosamente
dorme; e il sonno, affannoso anche, gli giova,
l'insonnia una stanchezza in me rinnova,
che l'orgoglio mi fa quasi piacente.

Meraviglia non è se la mia mente
veglia, ed il sonno non sempre ritrova.
Questa che giace e ronfia è gente nuova.
Io sono vecchio, paurosamente.

Esistere da tanti anni mi sembra,
che forse con Abramo ho trasmigrato.
Forse fui Faust, e Margherita ho amato.

Qui coi conscritti oggi stancai le membra.
Ma non vissi con altri uomini e dèi?
Non videro ogni tempo gli occhi miei?

After the Silence

While my companion moaning lies asleep,
and sleep, though labored, always does him good,
a weariness revives with my insomnia,
which in my pride I almost relish.

It's no surprise my mind is still awake
and cannot find a way to sleep.
These people lying and snoring around me
are new; I am frighteningly old.

I feel I've been alive so many years,
I may well have gone forth with Abraham;
I may have been Faust, and loved Margarethe.

With these soldiers here today I wearied my bones.
But have I not lived with other men and gods?
Have my eyes not seen every age of man?

from

CASA E CAMAGNA

HOUSE AND COUNTRY

(1909-1910)

L'arboscello

Oggi il tempo è di pioggia.
Sembra il giorno una sera,
sembra la primavera
un autunno, ed un gran vento devasta
l'arboscello che sta – e non pare – saldo;
par tra le piante un giovanetto alto
troppo per la sua troppo verde età.
Tu lo guardi. Hai pietà
forse di tutti quei candidi fiori
che la bora gli toglie; e sono frutta,
sono dolci conserve
per l'inverno quei fiori che tra l'erbe
cadono. E se ne duole la tua vasta
maternità.

The Sapling

Rainy weather today.
Day seems like evening,
spring seems like autumn,
a fierce wind wreaks havoc
on a sapling that, despite appearances,
stands firm. Alongside all the other plants
it looks like a boy too tall for his green age.
You watch it and feel pity,
perhaps for all the white flowers
the North wind has stripped from its branches.
They are fruit, sweet preserves
for the winter, those flowers falling
to the grass. Vast in its grief is your
motherhood.

A mia moglie

Tu sei come una giovane,
una bianca pollastra.
Le si arruffano al vento
le piume, il collo china
per bere, e in terra raspa;
ma, nell'andare, ha il lento
tuo passo di regina,
ed incede sull'erba
pettoruta e superba.
È migliore del maschio.
È come sono tutte
le femmine di tutti
i sereni animali
che avvicinano a Dio.
Così se l'occhio, se il giudizio mio
non m'inganna, fra queste hai le tue uguali,
e in nessun'altra donna.
Quando la sera assonna
le gallinelle
mettono voci che ricordan quelle,
dolcissime, onde a volte dei tuoi mali,
ti quereli, e non sai
che la tua voce ha la soave e triste
musica dei pollai.

Tu sei come una gravida
giovenca;
libera ancora e senza
gravezza, anzi festosa;
che, se la lisci, il collo
volge, ove tinge un rosa
tenero la sua carne.
Se l'incontri e muggire
l'odi, tanto è quel suono
lamentoso, che l'erba
strappi, per farle un dono.
È così che il mio dono
t'offro quando sei triste.

To My Wife

You are like
a young white hen,
with feathers ruffled
in the wind, who bends her neck
to drink and scratch the ground
yet walks with your same slow
and queenly step,
proud and puffed-up
as she struts onto the grass.
She is better than the male.
She is like all
the females of all
the peaceful animals
living close to God.
So if my eye does not deceive me,
if my judgement is correct, it is in their number
that you find your equals,
and in no other woman.
When evening comes to lull
the chickens all to sleep,
they coo in voices that recall
the sweet sounds you sometimes make
when ailing, unaware
you're echoing the sad and gentle
music of the hen-house.

You are like a pregnant
heifer,
still roaming free and still
unburdened, frolicsome, in fact,
who when you stroke her
bends her neck toward you,
the skin beneath a tender pink.
And if sometime you hear her
moo, so plaintive is the sound
of it, you tear the grass up from the ground
and give it to her as a gift.
So, too, do I offer you
my gifts when you feel sad.

Tu sei come una lunga
cagna, che sempre tanta
dolcezza ha negli occhi,
e ferocia nel cuore.
Ai tuoi piedi una santa
sembra, che d'un fervore
indomabile arda,
e così ti riguarda
come il suo Dio e Signore.
Quando in casa o per via
segue, a chi solo tenti
avvicinarsi, i denti
candidissimi scopre.
Ed il suo amore soffre
di gelosia.

Tu sei come la pavida
coniglia. Entro l'angusta
gabbia ritta al vederti
s'alza,
e verso te gli orecchi
alti protende e fermi;
che la crusca e i radicchi
tu le porti, di cui
priva in sé si rannicchia,
cerca gli angoli bui.
Chi potrebbe quel cibo
ritoglierle? chi il pelo
che si strappa di dosso,
per aggiungerlo al nido
dove poi partorire?
Chi mai farti soffrire?

Tu sei come la rondine
che torna in primavera.
Ma in autunno riparte;
e tu non hai quest'arte.
Tu questo hai della rondine:
le movenze leggere;
questo che a me, che mi sentiva ed era
vecchio, annunciavi un'altra primavera.

You are like a lanky
dog, with eyes so
full of tenderness,
such fierceness in her heart.
At your feet she seems
a saint, burning with
untamable devotion,
looks up at you
as at her Lord and God.
When following close behind,
at home or on the street,
to all who so much as approach
she bares her pure white teeth.
Hers is a love disturbed
by jealousy.

You are like the timid
rabbit, who in her narrow
cage stands straight up
at the sight of you,
and toward you turns
her long, unmoving ears,
waiting for the bran and chicory
you bring to her. If left unfed
she huddles up into herself,
seeks out dark corners.
But who could ever deny her
that food? Who could ever
strip her of the fur she plucks
from her own skin to build the nest
where she will bear her young?
Who could ever do you harm?

You are like the swallow
that returns each year in spring;
but then she leaves again in autumn,
and you're not like that at all.
What makes you like the swallow
are your graceful movements,
and that you heralded, to one who felt
and was so old as I, another spring.

Tu sei come la provvida
formica. Di lei, quando
escono alla campagna,
parla al bimbo la nonna
che l'accompagna.
E così nella pecchia
ti ritrovo, ed in tutte
le femmine di tutti
i sereni animali
che avvicinano a Dio;
e in nessun'altra donna.

You are like the wise, far-seeing
ant, that a grandmother might
hold up as an example
to her grandson
while on a country walk.
And in the honeybee
I see you too, and in all
the females of all
the peaceful animals
living close to God;
and in no other woman.

L'insonnia in una notte d'estate

Mi sono messo a giacere
sotto le stelle,
una di quelle
notti che fanno dell'insonnia tetra
un religioso piacere.
Il mio guanciale è una pietra.

Siede, a due passi, un cane.
Siede immobile e guarda
sempre un punto, lontano.
Sembra quasi che pensi,
che sia degno di un rito,
che nel suo corpo passino i silenzi
dell'infinito.

Di sotto un cielo così turchino,
in una notte così stellata,
Giacobbe sognò la scalata
d'angeli di tra il cielo e il suo guanciale,
ch'era una pietra.
In stelle innumerevoli il fanciullo
contava la progenie sua a venire;
in quel paese ove fuggiva l'ire
del più forte Esaù,
un impero incrollabile nel fiore
della ricchezza per i figli suoi;
e l'incubo del sogno era il Signore
che lottava con lui.

A Summer Night's Insomnia

I lay myself down
under the stars,
on one of those nights
that make wretched sleeplessness
one of life's sacred pleasures.
A stone is my pillow.

A few steps away sits a dog.
He sits without moving, gazing
out at some point far away.
He seems almost to be thinking,
as if in some solemn rite,
as if his body were the vessel
of eternal silence.

Under just such a deep-blue sky,
on just such a starry night,
Jacob dreamed of a ladder of angels
leading up to the sky from his pillow,
which was a stone.
In the endless stars the young man
counted his future descendants;
in the land he had come to,
fleeing the stronger Esau,
he saw an invincible empire
of riches for his sons and heirs;
and in his dream the nightmare was the Lord,
who was wrestling with him.

Il maiale

La broda, fior di sudiciume, è pura
solo quanto il suo istinto n'è affamato:
strilla come il bambino sculacciato,
se allontani da lui la sua lordura.

Certo per lui grande ventura è quello
che per me, per un mio pensiero, è strazio:
che non si chieda perchè lo vuol bello
di pinguedine, e il più pasciuto e sazio,
la massaia che scaccia il poverello;
ch'egli, come ogni vita, ignori a cosa
poi gioverà quando sarà perfetto.
Ma io, se riguardando in lui mi metto,
io sento nelle sue carni il coltello,
sento quell'urlo, quella spaventosa
querela quando al gruppo un cane abbaia
e la massaia ride dalla soglia.

Solo in me mette un impetuosa voglia
di piangere quel suo beato aspetto.

The Pig

The swill, flower of filth, is only pure
as his instinctive hunger for it.
If you take that slop away from him
he shrieks like a child just spanked.

Of course, what for him is a great boon
is for me, to my way of thinking, a torment:
he does not wonder why the farmer's wife,
who chases the poor thing about the yard,
wants him nice and fat, well-fed as can be.
Like all life he does not know what purpose
he will serve when he has reached perfection.
Yet if I look at him and put myself
inside his skin, I feel the knife cut through
the flesh, I feel that scream, that horrible
lament, as the dog barks at the crowd,
and the farmer's wife laughs from the doorway.

I alone, to see his beatific gaze,
feel an overwhelming desire to weep.

La capra

Ho parlato a una capra.
Era sola sul prato, era legata.
Sazia d'erba, bagnata
dalla pioggia, belava.

Quell'uguale belato era fraterno
al mio dolore. Ed io risposi, prima
per celia, poi perché il dolore è eterno,
ha una voce e non varia.
Questa voce sentiva
gemere in una capra solitaria.

In una capra dal viso semita
sentiva querelarsi ogni altro male,
ogni altra vita.

The Goat

I had a conversation with a goat.
She was tied up, alone, in a field.
Full up with grass, wet
with rain, she was bleating.

That monotonous bleat was brother
to my own pain. And I replied in kind, at first
in jest, and then because pain is eternal
and speaks with one voice, unchanging.
This was the voice I heard
wailing in a lonely goat.

In a goat with a Semitic face
I heard the cry of every woe on earth,
every life on earth.

from

TRIESTE E UNA DONNA

TRIESTE AND A WOMAN

(1910-1912)

Città vecchia

Spesso, per ritornare alla mia casa
prendo un'oscura via di città vecchia.
Giallo in qualche pozzanghera si specchia
qualche fanale, e affollata è la strada.

Qui tra la gente che viene che va
dall'osteria alla casa o al lupanare,
dove son merci ed uomini il detrito
di un gran porto di mare
io ritrovo, passando, l'infinito
nell'umiltà.
Qui prostituta e marinaio, il vecchio
che bestemmia, la femmina che bega,
il dragone che siede alla bottega
del friggitore,
la tumultuante giovane impazzita
d'amore,
sono tutte creature della vita
e del dolore;
s'agita in esse, come in me, il Signore.

Qui degli umili sento in compagnia
il mio pensiero farsi
più puro dove più turpe è la via.

Old Town

Often when I'm walking home I'll go
by way of some dark street in the old town.
The thoroughfares are crowded, the streetlamps
shine in puddles with a yellow glow.

Here, among the men that come and go
between tavern and home or the brothel,
where goods and people are the petty
flotsam of a great sea port,
I in passing find eternity
in wretchedness.
Here the prostitute, the sailor, the old man
shouting curses, the woman in a rage,
the dragoon eating fritters
sitting in a store,
the lovesick adolescent girl
who wants to be adored,
all are creatures of this world
and its reward
of sorrow; and in them all, and me, there moves the Lord.

Here, when in the presence of the lowly,
I feel my thoughts
in streets of greatest squalor grow most holy.

Tre vie

C'è a Trieste una via dove mi specchio
nei lunghi giorni di chiusa tristezza:
si chiama Via del Lazzaretto Vecchio.
Tra case come ospizi antiche uguali,
ha una nota, una sola, d'allegrezza:
il mare in fondo alle sue laterali.
Odorata di droghe e di catrame
dai magazzini desolati a fronte,
fa commercio di reti, di cordame
per le navi: un negozio ha per insegna
una bandiera; nell'interno, volte
contro il passante, che raro le degna
d'uno sguardo, coi volti esangui e proni
sui colori di tutte le nazioni,
le lavoranti scontano la pena
della vita: innocenti prigioniere
cuciono tetre le allegre bandiere.

A Trieste ove son tristezze molte,
e bellezze di cielo e di contrada,
c'è un'erta che si chiama Via del Monte.
Incomincia con una sinagoga,
e termina ad un chiostro; a mezza strada
ha una cappella; indi la nera foga
della vita scoprire puoi da un prato,
e il mare con le navi e il promontorio,
e la folla e le tende del mercato.
Pure, a fianco dell'erta, è un camposanto
abbandonato, ove nessun mortorio
entra, non si sotterra piú, per quanto
io mi ricordi: il vecchio cimitero
degli ebrei, così caro al mio pensiero,
se vi penso i miei vecchi, dopo tanto
penare e mercatare, là sepolti,
simili tutti d'animo e di volti.

Three Streets

In Trieste there's a street in which I see myself
reflected, on long days of sequestered gloom:
it's called Via del Lazzaretto Vecchio.
Among old houses all alike as hospices,
there is but a single note of happiness:
the sea at the end of its side-streets.
Smelling of spices and tar from inside
the dark warehouses with their shabby façades,
the Via does business in fishnets and cables
for ships. One store has a banner
for a sign; inside, turned toward
the passersby, who rarely deign to look
at them, the workwomen, faces pale
and bending over the colors
of all nations, serve out the sentence
of life: innocent prisoners all,
they grimly sew their cheerful banners.

In Trieste, a city of much sorrow
and great beauty of landscape and sky,
there is a steep road we know as Via del Monte.
It begins with a synagogue
and ends with a cloister; halfway up
there is a chapel, and from a patch of grass
you can glimpse the dark rush of life below,
the sea with its ships and the headland,
the crowd and the tents in the market.
Next to this slope there is also an abandoned
graveyard, where no funerals are ever held.
They no longer bury anyone there, as far as I
can remember: it's the old cemetery
of the Jews, and I cherish it in memory
whenever I think of my forebears lying there
after lifetimes of suffering and trade,
all of like mind and appearance.

Via del Monte è la via dei santi affetti,
ma la via della gioia e dell'amore
è sempre Via Domenico Rossetti.
Questa verde contrada suburbana,
che perde dì per dì del suo colore,
che è sempre più città, meno campagna,
serba il fascino ancora dei suoi belli
anni, delle sue prime ville sperse,
dei suoi radi filari d'alberelli.
Chi la passeggia in queste ultime sere
d'estate, quando tutte sono aperte
le finestre, e ciascuna è un belvedere,
dove agucchiando o leggendo si aspetta,
pensa che forse qui la sua diletta
rifiorirebbe all'antico piacere
di vivere, di amare lui, lui solo;
e a più rosea salute il suo figliolo.

Via del Monte is the street of sacred sentiment,
but the street of love and merriment
is still Via Domenico Rossetti.
This green suburban avenue
loses color with each passing day,
ever more city, ever less country.
Still it preserves the charm of the days
of its youth, of the first secluded villas,
the straggly rows of saplings. Anyone
who walks along it on these final summer
evenings—when the windows are all open
and at each one sits, as on a lookout,
a lady idly sewing or reading—
will think that here, perhaps, his beloved
could reblossom to the ancient pleasure
of living, of loving him and him alone—
and his son awaken strong of flesh and bone.

Il poeta

Il poeta ha le sue giornate
contate,
come tutti gli uomini; ma quanto,
quanto variate!

L'ore del giorno e le quattro stagioni,
un po' meno di sole o più di vento,
sono lo svago e l'accompagnamento
sempre diverso per le sue passioni
sempre le stesse; ed il tempo che fa
quando si leva, è il grande avvenimento
del giorno, la sua gioia appena desto.
Sovra ogni aspetto lo rallegra questo
d'avverse luci, le belle giornate
movimentate
come la folla in una lunga istoria,
dove azzurro e tempesta poco dura,
e si alternano messi di sventura
e di vittoria.
Con un rosso di sera fa ritorno,
e con le nubi cangia di colore
la sua felicità,
se non cangia il suo cuore.

Il poeta ha le sue giornate
contate,
come tutti gli uomini; ma quanto,
quanto beate!

The Poet

The poet has just so many days
to live,
like every one of us, yet so many ways
to live them!

The hours of the day and the year's four seasons,
some with less sun or a little more wind,
are just so many amusements, so many reasons,
all different, for finding his passions
embodied in things. The weather outside
when he gets out of bed is the day's main
event, his joy when he opens his eyes.
But of all these things what most satisfies
him are the contests of light, the beautiful days
that always amaze
like the characters in a long history,
where blue skies soon vary with storm and rain
and life serves up in alternation pain
and victory.
As evening turns to red his happiness
returns, changes color in reflection
of the clouds,
but never changes his affection.

The poet has just so many days
to live,
like every one of us, and yet what days
of blessedness!

Il bel pensiero

Avevo un bel pensiero, e l'ho perduto.
Uno di quei pensieri che tra il sonno
e la veglia consolano la casta
adolescenza; e ben di rado poi
fan ritorno fra noi.

Io perseguivo il mio pensiero come
si persegue una bella creatura,
che ne conduce ove a lei piace, ed ecco:
perdi per sempre la sua leggiadria
a una svolta di via.

Una voce profana, un importuno
richiamo il bel pensiero in fuga han messo.
Ora lo cerco in ciechi labirinti
d'inferno, e so ch'esser non può lontano,
ma che sperarlo è vano.

The Good Thought

I had a good thought and then lost it.
It was one of those thoughts between sleep
and waking that comfort our chaste
adolescence—and then
hardly ever come back.

I pursued my thought as
one pursues a splendid creature
that leads you wherever she pleases
before her charm forever vanishes
round a bend in the road.

An irreverent voice, an irksome
shout, put my good thought to flight.
Now I look for it in the blind mazes
of hell. I know it can't be far off,
but it is useless to hope.

Nuovi versi alla Lina

1

Una donna! E a scordarla ancor m'aggiro
io per il porto, come un levantino.
Guardo il mare: ha perduto il suo turchino,
e a vuoto il mondo ammiro.

Una donna, una ben piccola cosa,
una cosa – Dio mio! – tanto meschina;
poi una come lei, sempre più ascosa.
in se stessa, che pare ogni mattina
occupi meno spazio a questo mondo,
dare ad un'esistenza il suo profondo
dolore; solo io qui sentirmi e sperso,
se piùdi lei la mia città non riempio;
spoglio per essa, e senz'altare, il tempio
dell'universo.

Una donna, un nonnulla. E i giorni miei
sono tristi; una donna ne fa strazio,
piccola, che una casa nello spazio,
un piroscafo è tanto piùdi lei.

New Lines for Lina

1

A woman! And to forget her I still wander
about the port, like a Levantine. I look
at the sea. It has lost its midnight blue;
in emptiness I marvel at the world.

A woman, a petty little thing,
my God! a wretched thing indeed.
And then one like her, ever more concealed
inside herself, who every morning seems
to take up less room in the world,
to give a life its due in sorrow.
While I alone here am at wits' end
if I can't fill my city more than she.
Bare and without altar, for her, is the temple
of the universe.

A woman, a non-entity. And my days
are full of sadness, brought to ruin
by a woman, one so small a steamship
or a house is much, much more than she.

2

Quando il rimorso ti dà troppe pene,
e in fretta mandi mie nuove a sentire;
vorrei pure rispondere: Sto bene;
ma che giova mentire?

Per amor tuo, per tua tranquillità
di fingermi felice anche ho pensato;
ma tu molto hai vissuto e sai se v'ha
pace in questo mio stato.

Pure non t'odio; e solo una preghiera
volgo, per tanta sconoscenza, a Dio:
che sappi un dì che immensa cosa egli era
questo vecchio amor mio.

2

When your remorse becomes too much to bear,
and in haste you send for news of me,
I wish I could reply: I'm fine.
But what good is it to lie?

For love of you, to set your mind at rest,
I've even thought of feigning happiness.
But you've lived long enough to know what peace
there is in my condition.

But I don't hate you; and of God I ask
one thing alone for such ingratitude:
I pray that you might one day know how vast
was this old love of mine.

3

Se dopo notti affannose mi levo
che l'angoscia dei sogni ancor mi tiene,
e se da quello il mio male mi viene
che più in alto ponevo;

se in ogni strada che vidi sì bella
vedo adesso una via del cimitero,
e della mia stanzetta il tuo pensiero
mi fa un'orrida cella;

quel giorno ancora chiamo il più felice
dei miei giorni, che in rosso scialle avvolta
ho salutata per la prima volta
Lina la cucitrice.

3

Though I may rise from troubled nights
still trapped inside the anguish of my dreams,
and though my torment now should come from what
I once held highest in esteem;

though every street that once was beautiful
to me I now see leading to the graveyard,
and the thought of you now turns my room
into a horrid cell;

still the day I call the happiest
of all my life, was when I first
said hello to Lina the seamstress,
wrapped in her red shawl.

4

Ora se in strada accanto a me ti sento
(sia vero o falso) tosto il passo affretto;
eppure credi che non io pavento
ricevere quel colpo in mezzo al petto.

Mi rivedi in un mese già invecchiato;
ma temo non sia solo il viver mio
che come il fazzoletto dell'addio
sarà tutto di lacrime impregnato.

Calpestato tu l'hai questo mio cuore!
Ma di una donna non sa far vendetta.
È abitato da Dio, pieno d'amore;
nei miei sogni ti chiamo benedetta.

4

Now when on the street I feel you there
beside me (whether you're there or not), I
quicken my step. You think I'm not afraid
to take that blow square in the chest.

You'll see me in a month, already older;
but I fear that mine is not the only life
that, like handkerchiefs waving goodbye,
will be all wet with tears.

You have trampled on this heart of mine!
But on a woman it could never take revenge.
It's inhabited by God, and full of love;
and in my dreams I call you blest.

13

Dico al mio cuore, intanto che t'aspetto:
Scordala, che sarà cosa gentile.
Ti vedo, e generoso in uno e vile,
a te m'affretto.

So che per quanto alla mia vita hai tolto,
e per te stessa dovrei odiarti.
Ma poi altro che un bacio non so darti
quando t'ascolto.

Quando t'ascolto parlarmi d'amore
sento che il male ti lasciava intatta;
sento che la tua voce amara è fatta
per il mio cuore.

13

To my heart I say, as I await you:
Forget her, that would be the finer thing.
Then I see you, and feeling at once generous
and craven, I rush to you.

I should hate you, I know, for all that
you've taken from me, just for being you.
But I don't know what to do but kiss you
when I hear you speak.

When I hear you speak to me of love,
I can tell the pain has left you whole,
I can hear your bitter voice is made
only for my heart.

15

Un marinaio di noi mi parlava,
di noi fra un ritornello di taverna.
Sotto l'azzurra blusa una fraterna
pena a me l'uguagliava.

La sua storia d'amore a me narrando,
sparger lo vidi una lacrima sola.
Ma una lacrima d'uomo, una, una sola,
val tutto il vostro pianto.

"Quell'uomo ed uno come te, ma come
posson sedere assieme all'osteria?"
Ed anche per dir male, Lina mia,
delle povere donne.

15

A sailor was telling me about us,
about us, between a tavern-song's refrains.
Underneath his light-blue shirt a common pain
made him just like me.

As he told me the story of his love,
I saw him shed a single tear.
But a man's tear, even just one,
is worth all your weeping.

"But how could you ever sit down
at the same table with a man like that?"
And it was even, dear Lina, to speak ill
of you poor women.

from

LA SERENA DISPERAZIONE

SERENE DESPERATION

(1913-15)

Un ricordo

Non dormo. Vedo una strada, un boschetto,
che sul mio cuore come un'ansia preme;
dove si andava, per star soli e insieme,
io e un altro ragazzetto.

Era la Pasqua; i riti lunghi e strani
dei vecchi. E se non mi volesse bene
– pensavo – e non venisse più domani?
E domani non venne. Fu un dolore,
uno spasimo fu verso la sera;
che un'amicizia (seppi poi) non era,
era quello un amore;

il primo; e quale e che felicità
n'ebbi, tra i colli e il mare di Trieste.
Ma perché non dormire, oggi, con queste
storie di, credo, quindici anni fa?

A Memory

I can't sleep. I see a street, a thicket
that weighs heavy as a worry on my chest;
it's a place we used to go to, another
boy and I, to be together and alone.

It was Easter, with all the strange,
long rituals of the grown-ups. But what if
he doesn't really like me, I thought, and doesn't come back
tomorrow? And tomorrow he didn't come back.
It hurt, and by evening my heart ached.
For what we had (I know now) was not friendship:
it was love.

My first. And how happy it made me,
between the hills and the sea of Trieste.
But why lose sleep today, with things
that happened, I believe, some fifteen years ago?

Guido

1

Sul campo, ove a frugar tra l'erba siede,
mi scorge, e in fretta a sé mi chiama, o impronto
s'appressa, come chi un compagno vede;

sciocchissimo fanciullo, a cui colora
le guance un rosa di nubi al tramonto,
e ai quindici anni non par giunto ancora.

Parla di nevicate e di radicchi,
e del paese ove ha uno zio bifolco.
Poi, senza ch'altri lo rincorra o picchi,

fugge da me che intento l'ho ascoltato;
or lo guardo tenersi bene al solco,
non mai, correndo, entrar nel seminato.

Giunto al cancello, lo vedrò in quel tratto
tornarmi, se non fa il verso al tacchino,
o non mi scorda per l'amor che ratto

nasce tra un cane giovane e un bambino.

Guido

1

From the field where he sits poking through the grass,
he spots me, calls me hurriedly to him
or comes rushing up, as when one sees a friend.

Foolish boy, with cheeks the rosy color
of the clouds at sunset, he doesn't
even look fifteen years old.

He talks of snowfalls and chicory and the town
where his ploughman uncle lives.
Then suddenly he flees from me, his intent

listener, though no one comes for him or threatens
punishment. I watch him as he nimbly runs
along the furrow, not once treading seeded ground.

Once he's at the gate, I see him turning round
toward me, unless he's gobbling at the turkey
or has forgotten me amid the raptures

of a love between a young dog and a boy.

2

Ma spesso, per dovere o per trastullo,
come un buon padre o un amoroso balio,
conduce a mano un piccolo fanciullo.

E i giorni di lavoro nè s'aggira
pei campi, nè alla scuola è il suo travaglio.
La mamma sua fuor del caldo lo tira,

assonnato lo manda afl'officina;
non vede come ai giovanetti è bello
di primavera dormir la mattina.

Là un po' s'annoia, un po' ride schiamazza;
che il mastro, o un più di lui grosso monello
lo insegue in una lunga corsa pazza.

Chi lo giunge lo mette rovescioni,
e se lo serra fra i duri ginocchi.
Ride il vinto, trattato a sculaccioni,

e ridendo si sente punger gli occhi.

2

Sometimes, as a chore or just for fun, he'll show up
hand in hand, like a doting father
or fond guardian, with a small boy in his charge.

On workdays he is never to be seen about
the fields, nor was he made for schoolwork.
To keep him out of the hot sun, his mother

sends him half-asleep to work in the shop.
She doesn't understand how nice it is for boys
to sleep late mornings in the spring.

And there he gets a little bored, sometimes he laughs
and shouts, and the shop foreman, or some bigger
stripling, chases wildly after him.

The one who catches hold of him throws him
on his back, clamps him tight between hard knees.
The loser laughs and gets a spanking,

and laughing feels his eyes begin to burn.

3

Guido ha qualcosa dell'anima mia,
dell'anima di tante creature
e tiene in cuore la sua nostalgia.

Gli dico: "Non verrai con me a Trieste?
Là c'è il mestiere per tutti, e c'è pure
da divertirsi domeniche e feste".

"Laggiù dove ci son – dice – gli slavi?"
"Vedessi – dico – la bella montagna,
e il mar dove d'aprile già ti lavi."

"E a Tripoli – risponde – c'è mai stato?";
e si piega a frugar tra l'erbaspagna,
e a mostrarmi un radicchio che ha strappato.

"Vedessi i nuovi bastimenti, il molo
di sera" . . . e vedo irradiarsi in volto
Guido, che vuol andare, oh sì, ma solo

a Cassalecchio, ove ha uno zio bifolco.

3

Guido's a little like me in spirit,
a little like many other creatures:
he keeps his yearning to himself.

"Won't you come with me to Trieste?" I ask him.
"There's work for everyone there, and on Sundays
and holidays there are good times to be had."

"You mean the city where the Slavs live?" he says.
"You should see the pretty mountains," say I,
"and the sea, where you can swim as soon as April."

"And Tripoli," he says, "have you ever been there?"
and he bends down to poke about the Spanish clover,
and shows me some chicory he's pulled up.

"You should see the bright new ships, the docks
at night . . ." and suddenly I see his face light up.
He'd like to go, oh yes, but just to Casalecchio,

where his ploughman uncle lives.

from

COSE LEGGERE E VAGANTI

LIGHT AND AIRY THINGS

(1920)

Ritratto della mia bambina

La mia bambina con la palla in mano,
con gli occhi grandi colore del cielo
e dell'estiva vesticciola: "Babbo
—mi disse—voglio uscire oggi con te."
Ed io pensavo: Di tante parvenze
che s'ammirano al mondo, io ben so a quali
posso la mia bambina assomigliare.
Certo alla schiuma, alla marina schiuma
che sull'onde biancheggia, a quella scia
ch'esce azzurra dai tetti e il vento sperde;
anche alle nubi, insensibili nubi
che si fanno e disfanno in chiaro cielo;
e ad altre cose leggere e vaganti.

Portrait of My Daughter

With ball in hand and big round eyes the color
of the sky and of her pretty summer dress,
my little girl said to me: "Daddy,
today I want to go outside with you."
And I thought: Of all the images
to be admired in the world, I know well
the ones to which I may compare my little girl.
She is like foam, the white sea foam that floats
atop the waves, and like the plume that rises
light-blue from the rooftops and is scattered
by the wind, and like the clouds, the wispy clouds
that form and break up in the open sky,
and like so many other light and airy things.

Favoletta

Tu sei la nuvoletta, io sono il vento;
    ti porto ove a me piace;
qua e là ti porto per il firmamento,
    e non ti do mai pace.

Vanno a sera a dormire dietro i monti
    le nuvolette stanche.
Tu nel tuo letticciolo i sonni hai pronti
    sotti le coltri bianche.

Story

You are a little cloud, I am the wind,
      I take you wherever I please;
across the sky you twist and bend,
      ever at the mercy of the breeze.

At nightfall all the little clouds
      go behind the hills to sleep.
In your bed of soft white shrouds
      a ready nest of dreams you keep.

Paolina

Paolina, dolce
Paolina,
raggio di sole entrato nella mia
vita improvviso;
chi sei, che appena ti conosco e tremo
se mi sei presso? tu a cui ieri ancora
"Il suo nome—chiedevo—signorina?";
e tu alzando su me gli occhi di sogno
rispondevi: "Paolina."

Paolina, frutto
natio,
fatta di cose le più aeree e insieme
le più terrene,
nata ove solo nascere potevi,
nella città benedetta ove nacqui,
su cui vagano a sera i bei colori,
i più divini colori, e ahimè! sono
nulla; acquei vapori.

Paolina, dolce
Paolina,
che tieni in cuore? Io non lo chiedo. È pura
la tua bellezza;
vi farebbe un pensiero quel che un alito
sullo specchio, che subito s'appanna.
Qual sei mi piaci, aureolata testina,
una qualunque fanciulla e una Dea
che si chiama Paolina.

Paolina

Paolina, darling
Paolina,
ray of sunlight come into my life
to my surprise,
who are you? Though I hardly know you, still
I tremble when you're near—you to whom just yesterday
I asked, "Your name, young lady?"
and you looked up at me with dreamy eyes
and said: "Paolina."

Paolina, native
fruit,
made of the most airy things and also
the most earthly,
born where you could only have been born,
in the blessed city of my birth,
where pretty colors drift across the evening,
colors most divine, alas! they are
nothing, but air and water's leavening.

Paolina, darling
Paolina,
what stirs within your heart? I dare not ask. A beauty
pure as yours
a thought would only trouble,
as breath beclouds a looking-glass.
I like you as you are, halo round your little head,
a girl like any other and a goddess
by the name of Paolina.

from

L'AMOROSA SPINA

THE LOVING THORN

(1920)

1

Sento che in fondo ai miei pensieri, a queste
ore beate e meste,
sei tu, bambina.

Sei tu Chiaretta, che non son due anni,
non più brutta, non bella
più d'ogni altra monella,
in corti ancora sgraziati panni
ti s'incontrava per via, dalla mamma
per il pane mandata ed il carbone.
Ora sai sola quali a te son buone
cose: sul braccio reggi la borsetta,
chiudi in quella lo specchio, giovanetta
tu dai limpidi seni. E c'è lì dentro,

c'è quasi un cuore: uccelletto che a prova
canta un'antica e nuova
sua canzoncina.

1

At the back of my mind, in these
blissful gloomy hours, it's you
I find there, little girl.

It's you, Chiaretta, who barely two years ago,
no prettier or plainer
than any other tomboy
dressed in short, still shabby clothes,
we'd run into on the street, when your mother
sent you out for bread and coal.
Now all by yourself you know what serves you
best: you hold your small purse in your arms,
put your mirror in it, young lady
of gossamer breasts. And there inside,

there's almost a heart: a little bird that,
put to the test, sings an ancient, new song
all its own.

5

Nasca da un amor mio un fascicoletto
di versi, io pago sono.
Ho avuto un figlio teneto e diletto.

Un figlio di più lunga e meno mesta
vita che se di carne fosse, un buono
che a te pure dà pace.
Ma non nel cuore tu l'accogli; ahimè
l'omaggio solo è quello che ti piace;
che su tutte le cose tu di questa
godi: che molti soffrano per te;

e quanti più essi sono meglio è.

5

Let a little sheaf of verses spring
from my love, and I am happy.
A tender, darling child I have borne.

A son who'll live a life much longer
and less gloomy than if he were of flesh,
a good son who to you as well brings peace.
But in your heart you do not welcome him.
The homage alone, alas, is what you like.
What thrills you more than anything
is that many should suffer for your sake,

and the more there are, the better.

7

Come ho goduto tra la veglia e il sonno
   questa mattina!
Uomo ero ancora, ed ero la marina
   libera ed infinita.

Con le calme dorate e gli orizzonti
   lontani il mare.
Nel fondo ove non occhio può arrivare,
   e non può lo scandaglio,

una pietruzza per me, una cosina
   da nulla aveva.
Per lei sola fremeva ed arrideva
   l'azzurra immensità.

7

What joy I felt this morning between
      sleep and waking!
Still a man I was, and an expanse of sea,
      free and endless.

With calm and golden ocean waters,
      distant horizons.
Lying at the bottom, beyond the reach
      of eye or lead-line,

was a little pebble, there just for me,
      a trifling thing.
For it alone the great blue vastness
      shuddered and beamed.

12

Sovrumana dolcezza
io so, che ti farà i begli occhi chiudere
come la morte.

Se tutti i succhi della primavera
fossero entrati nel mio vecchio tronco,
per farlo rifiorire anche una volta,
non tutto il bene sentirei che sento
solo a guardarti, ad aver te vicina,
a seguire ogni tuo gesto, ogni modo
tuo di essere, ogni tuo piccolo atto.
E se vicina non t'ho, se a te in alta
solitudine penso, più infuocato
serpeggia nelle mie vene il pensiero
della carne, il presagio

dell'amara dolcezza,
che so che ti farà i begli occhi chiudere
come la morte.

12

A superhuman sweetness
will close, I know, your pretty eyes
as if in death.

If all the saps of spring
rose up inside my agèd trunk
to make it blossom one more time
I still would never feel the joy I feel
just seeing you, just having you beside me
and following your every gesture, your every
way of being, your every slightest act.
And when you're not beside me, when in deep
solitude I think of you, then hotter
burns within my veins the thought
of the flesh, the anticipation

of the bitter sweetness that
will close, I know, your pretty eyes
as if in death.

In riva al mare

Eran le sei del pomeriggio, un giorno
chiaro festivo. Dietro al Faro, in quelle
parti ove s'ode beatamente il suono
d'una squilla, la voce d'un fanciullo
che gioca in pace intorno alla carcasse
di vecchie navi, presso all'ampio mare
solo seduto; io giunsi, se non erro,
a un culmine del mio dolore umano.

Tra i sassi che prendevo per lanciare
nell'onda (ed una galleggiante trave
era il bersaglio), un coccio ho rinvenuto,
un bel coccio marrone, un tempo gaia
utile forma nella cucinetta,
con le finestre aperte al sole e al verde
della collina. E fino a questo un uomo
può assomigliarsi, angosciosamente.

Passò una barca con la vela gialla,
che di giallo tingeva il mare sotto;
e il silenzio era estremo. Io della morte
non desiderio provai, ma vergogna
di non averla ancora unica eletta,
d'amare più di lei io qualche cosa
che sulla superficie della terra
si muove, e illude col soave viso.

Seaside

It was six o'clock on a clear holiday
evening. Behind the Lighthouse, in a spot
where I could hear a lovely ringing
sound, the voice of a young boy playing
peacefully around the carcasses
of old ships, beside the sprawling sea,
I sat down alone and, if I am not mistaken,
reached a culmination of my human sorrow.

Among the stones I was picking up and
throwing into the waves (a floating piece of timber
was my target), I found a piece of earthenware,
a fine brown shard, once a happy, useful
form in a bright and sunny kitchen
with a window looking out on green hills. That,
I thought, was the most a man could ever
hope, in all his anguish, to resemble.

A boat with yellow sails passed by,
casting yellow on the sea beneath it.
An utter silence reigned. For death I felt
no longing, but shame for not yet having
chosen it my only destination,
for loving more than it some thing
that moves across the surface of the earth
and fools us with its gentle face.

VOLUME II

(1921-1932)

from

PRELUDIO E CONZONETTE

PRELUDIO E CANZONETTE

(1922-23)

Il canto di un mattino

Da te, cuor mio, l'ultimo canto aspetto,
e mi diletto a pensarlo fra me.

Del mare sulla riva solatia,
non so se in sogno o vegliando, ho veduto,
quasi ancor giovanetto, un marinaio.
La gomena toglieva alla colonna
dell'approdo, e oscillava in mar la conscia
nave, pronta a salpare.
E l'udivo cantare,
per se stesso, ma sì che la città
n'era intenta, ed i colli e la marina,
e sopra tutte le cose il mio cuore:
"Meglio—cantava—dire addio all'amore,
se nell'amor non è felicità".
Lieto appariva il suo bel volto; intorno
era la pace, era il silenzio; alcuno
né vicino scorgevo né lontano;
brillava il sole nel cielo, sul piano
vasto del mare, nel nascente giorno.

Egli è solo, pensavo; or dove mai
vuole approdar la sua piccola barca?
"Così, piccina mia, così non va"
diceva il canto, il canto che per via
ti segue; alla taverna, come donna
di tutti, l'hai vicino.
Ma in quel chiaro mattino
altro ammoniva quella voce; e questo
lo sai tu, cuore mio, che strane cose
ti chiedevi ascoltando: or se lontana
andrà la nave, or se la pena vana
non fosse, ed una colpa il mio esser mesto.
Sempre cantando, si affrettava il mozzo
alla partenza; ed io pensavo: È un rozzo
uomo di mare? O è forse un semidio?

Si tacque a un tratto, balzò nella nave;
chiara soave rimembranza in me.

Song of a Morning

From you, my heart, I await the final song,
and love to wonder what it will be.

In the sunshine, by the sea,
I don't know if in a dream or not, I saw
a sailor, a young man almost still a boy.
He was loosing a rope from a mooring-post,
while in the water rocked the sentient
boat, ready to set sail.
And I heard him singing,
to himself, yet his song enchanted
the entire city, the hills and the marina,
and my heart above all.
You'd better say goodbye to love, he sang,
if love can't bring you happiness.
His handsome face looked cheerful. All around
was only peace and silence; there was
no one, near or far, that I could see.
The sun shone in the sky, above the vast
expanse of sea, across the newborn day.

He's alone, I thought. But where could
he be going in that little boat?
That, my little one, that won't do,
went the song, the one that follows you
about the streets, comes up beside you
in the tavern, like everybody's girl.
Yet on that bright morning there was
something else that voice was telling me.
As you, my heart, well know, you asked yourself
strange questions as you listened: Will the boat
sail far away? And is the effort simply
pointless, and my gloom a kind of sin?

Still singing, the boatman quickly
weighed anchor. And I thought: Is he just
a common seaman? Or not perhaps a demigod?
He suddenly fell silent, leapt into the boat,
a clear and gentle memory in me.

from

AUTOBIOGRAPHIA

AUTOBIOGRAPHY

(1924)

2

Quando nacqui mia madre ne piangeva,
sola, la notte, nel deserto letto.
Per me, per lei che il dolore struggeva,
trafficavano i suoi cari nel ghetto.

Da sé il più vecchio le spese faceva,
per risparmio, e più forse per diletto.
Con due fiorini un cappone metteva
nel suo grande turchino fazzoletto.

Come bella doveva essere allora
la mia città: tutta un mercato aperto!
Di molto verde, uscendo con mia madre,

io, come in sogno, mi ricordo ancora.
Ma di malinconia fui tosto esperto;
unico figlio che ha lontano il padre.

2

When I was born my mother wept for me,
alone, at night, in the deserted bed.
For my sake and hers, since she felt so grieved,
her loved ones bought and sold things in the ghetto.

The old man used to do the shopping by himself,
to economize, or just because he liked to.
He'd buy a capon for two bits and wrap it
in his enormous dark blue handkerchief.

How beautiful my city must have been
back then: a great big open-air market!
I still remember all the green I saw,

as in a dream, when I went out with mother.
But I was soon to be well-schooled in sadness,
an only son with an absent father.

3

Mio padre è stato per me "l'assassino,"
fino ai vent'anni che l'ho conosciuto.
Allora ho visto ch'egli era un bambino,
e che il dono ch'io ho da lui l'ho avuto.

Aveva in volto il mio sguardo azzurrino,
un sorriso, in miseria, dolce e astuto.
Andò sempre pel mondo pellegrino;
più d'una donna l'ha amato e pasciuto.

Egli era gaio e leggeto; mia madre
tutti sentiva delta vita i pesi.
Di mano ei gli sfuggì come un pallone.

"Non somigliare"—ammoniva—a tuo padre ".
Ed io più tardi in me stesso lo intesi:
Eran due razze in antica tenzone.

3

To me my father was the "murderer,"
for the twenty years until I met him.
And then I saw that he was just a child,
and that what gift I have I got from him.

His face possessed the same blue gaze as mine,
and a smile sweet and cunning in its sorrow.
He was always roaming free about the world
and had known the love of many women.

He was light and cheerful, while my mother
felt the weight of all life's burdens.
He slipped from her grasp like a ball.

She would warn me: "Don't be like your father."
And later on, deep down, I understood:
The strife between their races was ancient.

La mia infanzia fu povera e beata
di pochi amici, di qualche animale;
con una zia benefica ed amata
come la madre, e in cielo Iddio immortale.

All'angelo custode era lasciata
sgombra, la notte, metà del guanciale;
mai più la cara sua forma ho sognata
dopo la prima dolcezza carnale.

Di risa irrefrenabili ai compagni,
e a me di strano fervore argomento,
quando alla scuola i versi recitavo;

tra fischi, cori, animaleschi lagni,
ancor mi vedo in quella bolgia, e sento
sola un'intima voce dirmi bravo.

4

My childhood was lonely and blest
with few friends and some animals,
a charitable aunt I loved as a mother,
and immortal God in the heavens above.

To my guardian angel I left, at night,
half my pillow free; but never did
his precious form come back to me in dreams
once I had tasted the sweetness of the flesh.

To friends it was a cause for raucous
laughter, to me a strange excitement
when I would read my verse aloud at school;

'mid hoots and choruses of animal laments
I still can see myself inside that pit,
can hear the voice within that says "Well done."

6

Ebbi allora un amico; a lui scrivevo
lunghe lettere come ad una sposa.
Per esse appresi che una grazia avevo,
e a tutti ancor, fuor che a noi due, nascosa.

Dolci e saggi consigli io gli porgevo,
e doni a tanta amicizia amorosa.
Sulle sue gote di fanciul vedevo
l'aurora in cielo dipinta di rosa.

Su quelle care chiome avrei voluto
por di mia mano l'alloro una sera
di gloria, e dir: Questo è l'amico mio.

Fede il destino a lui non ha tenuto,
o forse quale mi apparve non era.
Egli era bello e lieto come un dio.

6

Then I made a friend; and I wrote him
long letters, as if he were my bride.
In these I learned I had a certain charm,
still hidden to all, except the two of us.

I would give him tender, sweet advice,
and gifts in honor of our loving friendship.
On his boyish cheeks I used to see
the sunrise paint the morning rose.

I wished that on that precious head of hair,
one glorious evening, I myself could place
the laurel crown, and say: This is my friend.

Destiny did not keep faith with him.
Or perhaps he was not what he seemed to me.
He was blithe and handsome as a god.

9

Notte e giorno un pensiero aver coatto,
estraneo a me, non mai da me diviso;
questo m'accadde; nei terrori a un tratto
dell'inferno cader dal paradiso.

Come da questo spaventoso fatto
io non rimasi, ancor lo ignoro, ucciso.
Invece strinsi col dolore un patto,
l'accettai, con lui vissi viso a viso.

Vidi altri luoghi, ebbi novelli amici.
Strane cose da strani libri appresi.
Dopo quattro o cinque anni, a poco a poco,

non più quei giorni estatici e felici
ebbi, mai più; ma liberi, ed intesi
della vita e dell'arte ancora al gioco.

9

Night and day I had a thought, extraneous
to me and undesired, that forced its way
into my head—where suddenly I'd fall
down from heaven to the terrors of hell.

How it is that from a thing so frightful
I managed not to die, I still don't know.
I did, however, make a deal with pain:
I accepted it, lived with it face to face.

I visited new places, made new friends.
I learned strange things from strange books.
Four or five years later, little by little

the rapture and joy had gone from my days,
never to return; but now they were free,
and still given to the play of life and art.

12

Ed amai nuovamente; e fu di Lina
dal rosso scialle il piùdella mia vita.
Quella che cresce accanto a noi, bambina
dagli occhi azzurri, è dal suo grembo uscita.

Trieste è la città, la donna è Lina,
per cui scrissi il mio libro di più ardita
sincerita; né dalla sua fu fin'
ad oggi mai l'anima mia partita.

Ogni altro conobbi umano amore;
ma per Lina torrei di nuovo un'altra
vita, di nuovo vorrei cominciare.

Per l'altezze l'amai del suo dolore;
perché tutto fu al mondo, e non mai scaltra,
e tutto seppe, e non se stessa, amare.

12

And then I loved again. And it was all
for Lina of the red shawl, the great love
of my life. From her womb came the blue-eyed
little girl now growing up beside us.

Trieste is the city, Lina the woman
for whom I wrote my most courageously
heartfelt book; and never to this day
have our two souls been separated.

I have known every other human love;
but for Lina I would give up yet another
life; I would gladly start anew.

I loved her for the summits of her sorrow.
For she was everything, but never false,
and could love everything, but not herself.

15

Una strana bottega d'antiquario
s'apre, a Trieste, in una via secreta.
D'antiche legature un oro vario
l'occhio per gli scaffali errante allieta.

Vive in quell'aria tranquillo un poeta.
Dei morti in quel vivente lapidario
la sua opera compie, onesta e lieta,
d'Amor pensoso, ignoto e solitario.

Morir spezzato dal chiuso fervore
vorrebbe un giorno; sulle amate carte
chiudere gli occhi che han veduto tanto.

E quel che del suo tempo restò fuore
e del suo spazio, ancor più bello l'arte
gli pinse, ancor più dolce gli fe' il canto.

15

A strange antiquarian bookshop opens
in Trieste, on a secluded street.
On its shelves a sundry gold of age-
old bindings cheers the wandering eye.

In that quiet world there lives a poet.
And in that living showcase of the dead
he practices his honest, happy art,
with thoughts of Love, in solitude, unknown.

He'd like, one day, to die destroyed by his
reclusive fervor; to close his eyes,
so full of all they've seen, on his beloved papers.

And all that lay beyond his time and space
his art portrayed more beautifully
to him, his song made sweeter still.

from

I PRIGIONI

THE PRISONERS

(1924)

Il lussurioso

Ero, fanciullo, il primo in ogni ludo;
e sempre, come avessi avuto l'ale,
tendevo all'alto. Or tutto il bene e il male
in un pensiero che non dico chiudo.

Da me ogni gioia, fuori una, escludo
in cielo e in terra; al mio ardore mortale
il tronco è dato per castigo, al quale
Amore m'ha legato inerme ignudo.

Ahi, questi dispietati atroci nodi
m'entran sì dolci nella viva carne
che libertà, potendo, non torrei.

Più caro li stringesse in nuovi modi
Amore intorno alla mie membra, a farne
sprizzare il sangue giovanile, avrei.

The Man of Lust

As a boy I finished first in all the games;
I always aimed high, as if I had wings.
Now all good and evil dwell for me
in one thought alone, which I never express.

Every joy of heaven and earth but one
I deny myself. In punishment this trunk
is slave to my one mortal passion, to which
love has bound me, defenseless and naked.

Ah, the merciless, terrible knots
so sweetly pierce my living flesh that even
if I could, I would never remove them.

I'd have Love tighten them around my limbs
more tenderly, in new ways, if I could,
to spray my youthful blood about.

L'accidioso

La vita, non so bene in che, m'offese.
Ed io non chiedo più a lei che le cose
che son simili a morte. Gaudiose
io dico l'ore in cupi sonni spese.

Nasce l'uomo alla gloria, ad alte imprese,
a militare in schiere sanguinose.
Reo disgusto che in me Natura pose
tale, nel fiore degli anni, mi rese,

che far del giorno notte è il mio pensiero.
Ho in odio fin l'amorosa tenzone,
ed in occulto mi corrompo solo.

Fissa mia moglie in me il suo occhio
nero, dove sta scritta la mia dannazione;
e pietoso mi guarda il mio figliolo.

The Idler

Life, I don't quite know how, has wronged me.
I want nothing from it any more but
deathlike things. Long hours spent
in gloomy sleep for me are times of bliss.

Man is born for glory, for acts of greatness,
for fighting wars in bloody legions.
But in me Nature sowed a rank disgust
that makes my only wish, in bloom of youth,

to turn the daylight into night.
I even hold love's battle in contempt
and debase myself alone, in secret.

My wife's dark eyes stare hard at me.
In them I read my condemnation.
My young son looks at me with pity.

L'ispirato

Tutto, se lo spavento non m'atterra,
son luce. E tutte le cose create
vengon sì stranamente a me accoppiate
che il senso occulte rispondenze afferra.

Ma temo. Temo dei casi la guerra,
dell'uomo a me, alle in me imprigionate
forme, che a libertà reco. Giornate
troppo avrei dolci, senza questo, in terra.

Or d'amori inumani, or della sorte
pensoso, porto in me quasi ogni vita.
Tal dono e tal castigo ho ricevuto.

Non esser nato non vorrei, né morte
innanzi tempo; vorrei già compita
l'opera ch'è il mio Fato: esser vissuto.

The Genius

So long as terror does not knock me down,
I am all light. And all created things become
so strangely joined to me, my senses start
to grasp the world's occult relationships.

And yet I fear. I fear the war of accidents,
the man I liberate in me and in
the forms in me imprisoned. Too sweet
my days on earth would be, were this not so.

Concerned by turns with superhuman loves
and destiny, I hold most every life in me.
Such has been my gift and castigation.

My wish is not that I were never born,
nor dead before my time, but that I had already
done the work that is my fate: to have lived.

L'amante

Sul capo io porto un serto glorioso.
Amo una donna con cui mai non giacqui,
né mai mi giacerò, cui sempre tacqui
l'amor mio, che affissarla appena oso.

Ho su tutti in dispregio il Lussurioso.
Poiché, lode agli dèi, cotale io nacqui
che sempre e solo di quel mi compiacqui
che l'uomo fa nel giorno luminoso.

Come amerà una donna chi la sprezza
fino a corrompersi in lei? Di lei farmi
ho saputo una palma trionfale.

Veramente il mio nome è Giovanezza;
ma se un altro, o gentile, tu vuoi darmi,
chiamami il figlio di Teseo immortale.

The Lover

On my head I wear a crown of glory.
I love a woman whose bed I've not shared
and will never share, who knows nothing
of my love, on whom I scarcely dare to look.

Of all I most despise the Man of Lust.
For, the gods be praised, I was so made
that my only and eternal pleasure lies
in what man does by the light of day.

Can he love a woman who so despises her
as to debase himself in her?
In her I've found my victory palm.

Actually my name is Youth. But if you,
o gentle one, would call me by another,
call me son of immortal Theseus.

from

CUOR MORITURO

DYING HEART

(1925-30)

Il borgo

Fu nelle vie di questo
Borgo che nuova cosa
m'avvenne.

Fu come un vano
sospiro
il desiderio improvviso d'uscire
di me stesso, di vivere la vita
di tutti,
d'essere come tutti
gli uomini di tutti
i giorni.

Non ebbi io mai sì grande
gioia, né averla dalla vita spero.
Vent'anni avevo quella volta, ed ero
malato. Per le nuove
strade del Borgo il desiderio vano
come un sospiro
mi fece suo.

Dove nel dolce tempo
d'infanzia
poche vedevo sperse
arrampicate casette sul nudo
della collina,
sorgeva un Borgo fervente d'umano
lavoro. In lui la prima
volta soffersi il desiderio dolce
e vano
d'immettere la mia dentro la calda
vita di tutti,
d'essere come tutti
gli uomini di tutti
i giorni.

The Town

On the streets of this town
something new
came over me.

It was like an idle
wish
a sudden yearning to be outside
of myself, to live the life
of everyone,
to be like every
everyday
man.

I have never known a joy
so great, nor do I ever hope to.
I was twenty years old at the time,
and sick. And through the town's
new streets that idle yearning
like a wish
took hold of me forever.

Where in the gentle days
of childhood
I once saw little houses
scattered on the naked
hillside,
a town now stood, feverish with human
labor. It was there I first
suffered the sweet and idle
yearning
to join my own life with the warm
life of everyone,
to be like every
everyday
man.

La fede avere
di tutti, dire
parole, fare
cose che poi ciascuno intende, e sono,
come il vino ed il pane,
come i bimbi e le donne,
valori
di tutti. Ma un cantuccio,
ahimè, lasciavo al desiderio, azzurro
spiraglio,
per contemplarmi da quello, godere
l'alta gioia ottenuta
di non esser più io,
d'essere questo soltanto: fra gli uomini
un uomo.

Nato d'oscure
vicende,
poco fu il desiderio, appena un breve
sospiro. Lo ritrovo
—eco perduta
di giovanezza—per le vie del Borgo
mutate
più che mutato non sia io. Sui muri
dell'alte case,
sugli uomini e i lavori, su ogni cosa,
è sceso il velo che avvolge le cose
finite.

La chiesa è ancora
gialla, se il prato
che la circonda è meno verde. Il mare,
che scorgo al basso, ha un solo bastimento,
enorme,
che, fermo, piega da una parte. Forme,
colori,
vita onde nacque il mio sospiro dolce
e vile, un mondo
finito. Forme,
colori,
altri ho creati, rimanendo io stesso,
solo con il mio duro
patire. E morte
m'aspetta.

To have the same faith
as everyone else, to say
and do things
that are,
like bread and wine,
like women and children,
beloved
of all. But still, alas!
I left a little corner for my yearning, a chink
of blue sky
from which I might behold myself
and taste the joy
of no longer being myself
but only a man
among men.

Born of uncertain
events,
it was a modest yearning, barely
a moment's wish. Yet here it is again
— lost echo
of youth—in the very same town
whose streets have changed
far more than I. Over the walls
of tall tenements,
over the men and their labor and everything else,
a veil has fallen, the pall
of finite things.

The church is still
yellow, though the grass around it
not so green as before. On the sea below
I see but a single ship,
enormous,
immobile, and listing to one side. Shapes
and colors,
life that gave life to my sweet
and lowly yearning,
finite world. Other shapes
and colors
have I created, staying ever the same,
alone with my stubborn
affliction. And death
to look forward to.

Ritorneranno,
o a questo
Borgo, o sia a un altro come questo, i giorni
del fiore. Un altro
rivivrà la mia vita,
che in un travaglio estremo
di giovanezza, avrà pur egli chiesto,
sperato,
d'immettere la sua dentro la vita
di tutti,
d'essere come tutti
gli appariranno gli uomini di un giorno
d'allora.

To this same town
or to another
much like it, the days of bloom
shall return. Another
will relive my life,
and in the throes of youth
he too shall wish
and hope
to join his own life with that
of everyone,
to be as all men
will seem to him on that certain
distant day.

Favoletta

Il cane,
bianco sul bianco greto,
segue inquieto
un'ombra,

la nera
ombra d'una farfalla,
che su lui gialla
volteggia.

Ignara
ella del rischio, a scorno
gli voli intorno
parrebbe.

Ignara
gli viene, o astuta, addosso.
Egli di dosso
la scuote,

e volgesi
vorace all'ombra vana,
che si allontana
dal greto,

e sopra
un fiore, a suo costume,
rinchiude il lume
dell'ali.

Sappiate,
dilettissimi amici,
che nei felici
miei giorni,

ai giorni
che il mio, oggi arido, cuore
era all'amore
rinato,

Fable

A white dog
on white pebbles by the river
frantically pursues
a shadow,

the black
shadow of a butterfly
fluttering yellow
above him.

Unaware
of any risk, she seems to fly
about his head
in mockery.

Unaware
or artfully, she lands on him.
He shakes her off
his furry back

and turns about
ferociously to set upon
the empty shadow, which
now flies away

and settles
on a flower, as is her wont,
folding up the light
of her wings.

Be it known,
beloved friends, that years ago,
in days of happiness
now past,

when my heart,
now old and barren to the world,
was once again reborn
to love,

anch'io,
con preda più stupenda,
ebbi vicenda
uguale.

Ed era
bella! l'ultima cosa
che in me di rosa
si tinse.

Ed io,
io le lasciai sua vita;
io ne ho ghermita
un'ombra.

Sapevo
—sconsolata dolcezza—
ch'era saggezza
umana.

I myself
was in a story just like this one,
but with a quarry even more
stupendous.

And she was
beautiful! The final ember
to burst into flame
within me.

But I,
I let her have her life
and seized upon
a shadow.

And I knew
—joyless satisfaction—
such was the way
of wisdom.

Il Caffelatte

Amara
si sente. Quanto
più bramerebbe è quanto
non ha.

Bramerebbe, adorata
bambina,
potersi ancora un poco addormentare
un poco
sognare ancora ad occhi aperti. Poi
che piano piano entrasse una servente
antica, alla sua culla
devota,

che porge in tazza grata
bevanda.
Il latte vi ha sapor di menta alpina,
il nero
caffè un aroma d'oltremare. Invece
sta presso il letto la sua madre arcigna;
domestics miscela
le impone.

Bramerebbe, levata
sul tardi,
avere una stanzetta ove la vita
non entra
che come un vago sussurro. Una dolce
poltrona, un libro ad aspettarla sono;
un pensiero che tace
v'è forse.

Invece, con l'usata
rampogna,
a lei fa fretta la materna voce,
temuta
come il castigo sotto il quale, è un anno,
tra bianche coltri altro bianco scopriva.
Il non suo caffelatte
giú manda.

Caffelatte

Bitter
she wakes up. What she
desires most is what
she doesn't have.

She wishes, beloved
young thing,
she could sleep a little longer,
to daydream
yet a while in bed. And that
an ancient handmaid, devoted
to her care,

would enter softly, pour a cup
of welcome drink.
The milk would have a taste of Alpine mint,
the black
coffee a scent from beyond the sea. But
it's her sullen mother by her bed,
thrusting on her
some domestic brew.

She wishes she had a little room
of her own,
where she would sleep late and life
never entered
except in vague whispers. Where a gentle
armchair and a book awaited her,
and silent thought
perhaps.

But with the usual
reproach her mother's voice calls up to her
to hurry,
feared as the scourge under which she discovered,
last year, another white between white covers.
She swallows down the caffelatte
not her own.

Amara
si leva. E sente
che torna lentamente
felice.

Bitter,
she gets up. And slowly
starts to feel happy
again.

Eros

Sul breve palcoscenico una donna
fa, dopo il Cine, il suo numero.
                                    Applausi,
a scherno credo, ripetuti.
                                    In piedi,
dal loggione in un canto., un giovanetto,
mezzo spinto all'infuori, coi severi
occhi la guarda, che ogni tratto abbassa.
È fascino? È disgusto? È l'una e l'altra
cosa? Chi sa? Forse a sua madre pensa,
pensa se questo è l'amore. I lustrini,
sul gran corpo di lei, col gioco vario
delle luci l'abbagliano. E i severi
occhi riaperti, là più non li volge.
Solo ascolta la musica, leggera
musichetta da trivio, anche a me cara
talvolta, che per lui si è fatta, dentro
l'anima sua popolana ed altera,

una marcia guerriera.

Eros

On a small stage, after the movie,
a woman performs her act.
                              The crowd
applauds repeatedly, in mockery perhaps.
From the corner gallery, a young man
on his feet, hanging halfway out, looks
at her gravely, then turns his eyes away.
Is it fascination? Indignation? Or both?
Who knows? Perhaps he's thinking of his mother,
wondering if this is what love is.
                              Flashing
the stagelights about, the sequins on her
ample body dazzle him. And reopening
his dour eyes, he no longer looks her way.
He only listens to the music, a light
and vulgar sort of tune, the kind that I
myself am sometimes fond of, which in his
common, scornful soul has now become

a battle march.

Preghiera per una fanciulla povera

Erna, strana fanciulla, oscura come
la grazia.
                    Un giovane
l'amava, ed ella non poteva dargli,
per quanta pena gli facesse, un bacio.
Li dava a molti i dolci baci, a quello
che la pregava piangendo, nessuno.
Di lui fu sorte ammalarsi (da tempo
era senza lavoro, era da tempo
anche a sé un peso) e la fanciulla, finta
un'improvvisa passione, la bocca
dipinta
giungeva a quella del morente.
                                        Forse
ella può ancora guarire. Ma dove
cosa le accada di cui teme il freddo
questa fanciulla povera, Signore;
dove apparirti ella dovesse viso
a viso,

apri le porte del tuo paradiso.

Prayer for a Poor Young Girl

Erna, an odd girl, was mysterious
as grace.
              A young man
loved her dearly, but she could not bring herself
to kiss him, for all the pain it caused him.
Her sweet kisses she gave out to many, but
to the boy who pleaded tearfully, never.
As fate would have it, he grew ill
(he had long been without work, had long been
a burden even to himself), and the girl, feigning
sudden passion, pressed her
painted lips
to his near-lifeless mouth.
                          Perhaps
she will recover yet. But if
something whose cold she fears should befall
this poor girl, O Lord,
if she should appear before you
face to face,

open the gates of your heaven.

from

PRELUDIO E FUGHE

PRELUDE AND FUGUES

(1928-29)

Prima fuga (a 2 voci)

La vita, la mia vita, ha la tristezza
del nero magazzino di carbone,
che vedo ancora in questa strada. *Io vedo,*
per oltre alle sue porte aperte, il cielo
azzurro e il mare con le antenne. Nero
come là dentro è nel mio cuore; il cuore
dell'uomo è un antro di castigo. *È bello*
il cielo a mezzo la mattina, e bello
il mar che lo riflette, e bello è anch'esso
il mio cuore: uno specchio a tutti i cuori
viventi. Se nel mio guardo, se fuori
di lui, non vedo che disperazione,
tenebra, desiderio di morire,
cui lo spavento dell'ignoto a fronte
si pone, tutta la dolcezza a togliere
che quello in sé recherebbe. *Le foglie*
morte non fanno a me paura, e agli uomini
io penso come a foglie. Oggi i tuoi occhi,
del nero magazzino di carbone,
vedono il cielo ed il mare, al contrasto,
più luminosi: pensa che saranno
chiusi domani. *Ed altri s'apriranno,*
simili ai miei, simili ai tuoi. La vita,
la tua vita a te cara, è un lungo errore,
(breve, dorato, appena un'illusione!)
e tu lo sconti duramente. *Come*
in me in questi altri lo sconto: persone,
mansi animali affaticati; intorno
vadano in ozio o per faccende, io sono
in essi, ed essi sono in me e nel giorno
che ci rivela. Pascerti puoi tu
di fole ancora? Io soffro; il mio dolore,
lui solo, esiste. *E non un poco il blu*
del cielo, e il mare oggi sì unito, e in mare
le antiche vele e le ormeggiate navi,
e il nero magazzino di carbone,
che il quadro, come per caso, incornicia
stupendamente, e quelle più soavi

First Fugue (for 2 voices)

Life, my life, is joyless
as the black coal-cellar I still see
along this road. *Beyond its open doors*
I see the blue sky and a sea
of masts. It's black in there
as in my heart. Man's heart
is one great torture chamber. *The sky*
is beautiful mid-morning, the sea reflecting it
is beautiful, my heart itself
is beautiful—a mirror of all living
hearts. When all within my gaze
and all without is desperation,
darkness and wishing for death,
the fear of the unknown looms up
before me, and what sweetness the unknown
itself might hold is gone. *Dead leaves*
do not frighten me, and people are
as leaves to me. Today your eyes
see sky and sea beyond a black coal-
cellar, and are brighter for the contrast:
tomorrow they shall close forever.
And other eyes shall open to the world,
eyes like mine, like yours. Life, the life
you hold so dear, is one long mistake
(so brief and golden, barely an illusion!)
and we pay dearly for it. *I pay my part*
in me as in others—people, weary,
docile animals; though they may lie in idleness
or pass their days at work, still I live
in them and they in me, as in the daylight
that reveals us. Can you still live
on fairy tales? I suffer. My pain
alone exists. *And what about the blue*
of the sky and the sea so still today
and the ancient sails and ships at anchor
and the black coal-cellar that,
as if by chance, so splendidly frames
the picture, and the gentler things, apart from

cose che in te, del dolore al contrasto,
senti—accese delizie—e che non dici?
Troppo temo di perderle; felici
chiamo per questo i non nati. *I non nati
non sono, i morti non sono, vi è solo
la vita viva eternamente; il male
che passa e il bene che resta.* Il mio bene
passò, come il mio male, ma più in fretta
passò; di lui nulla mi resta. *Taci,
empie cose non dire. Anche tu taci,*
voce che dalla mia sei nata, voce
d'altri tempi serena; se puoi, taci;
lasciami assomiagliare la mia vita
—tetra cosa opprimente—a quella nera
volta, sotto alla quale un uomo siede,
fin che gli termini il giorno, e non vede
l'azzurro mare—*oh, quanta in te provavi
nel dir dolcezza!*—e il cielo che gli è sopra.

pain, you feel inside but don't express—keen
pleasures, those—do they exist?
I'm so afraid of losing them! For this
I call the unborn happy. *The unborn
do not exist. The dead do not exist. There
is only life, eternally alive. The bad
shall pass, the good remains.* The good for me
has passed, as has the bad, but faster
still. I've nothing left. *Quiet,
do not say ungodly things. You too be quiet,*
voice born of my own, serene voice
of another age, be quiet if you can.
Let us leave my life—dark, oppressive
thing—to its likeness as that blackened
vault, under which a man sits waiting
for his day to end, and does not see
the blue sea beyond—*oh what joy to say, as you
once did, oh joy!*—or the sky above.

Terza fuga (a 2 voci)

Mi levo come in un giardino ameno
un gioco d'acque;
che in un tempo, in un tempo più sereno,
mi piacque.

Il sole scherza tra le gocce e il vento
ne sparge intorno;
ma fu il diletto, il diletto ora spento
d'un giorno.

Fiorisco come al verde Aprile un prato
presso un ruscello.
Chi sa che il mondo non è che un larvato
macello,

come può rallegrarsi ai prati verdi,
al breve Aprile?
Se tu in un cieco dolore ti perdi,
e vile,

per te mi vestirò di neri panni,
e sarò triste.
La mia tristezza non farà ai tuoi danni
conquiste.

Ascolta, Eco gentile, ascolta il vero
che viene dietro,
che viene in fondo ad ogni mio pensiero
piùtetro.

Io lo so che la vita, oltre il dolore,
è più che un bene.

La angosce allora io ne dirò, il furore,
le pene;

che sono la tua Eco, ed il segreto
è in me delle tue paci.
Del tuo pensiero quello ti ripeto
che taci.

Third Fugue (for 2 voices)

I rise up like a splendid water jet
in a splendid garden,
which once, in less troubled times than these,
I used to like.

The sun plays gently through the drops the wind
sprays all about;
but it was only one day's pleasure,
now long gone.

I blossom like a meadow by a brook
in greening April.
If you know the world is but a secret
slaughterhouse,

how can you rejoice in greening meadows,
in fleeting April?
If you should lose yourself in blind and base
affliction,

for you I'll have to wear the black of grief,
and I shall suffer.
Your suffering will be no triumph
for my sadness.

Listen, sweet echo, listen to the truth
that follows fast,
that follows deep inside of every darkest
thought of mine.

I know well that life, beyond the pain,
is more than a gift.

Then trouble and anger and suffering
I'll speak of myself,

for I am your Echo, and in me lives
the secret of your peace.
What in your thoughts you choose to silence
I repeat.

Sesta fuga (a 3 voci)

1)   Io non so più dolce cosa
dell'amore in giovanezza,
di due amanti in lieta ebbrezza,
di cui l'un nell'altro muore.

Io non so più gran dolore
ch'esser privo di quel bene,
e non porto altre catene
di due braccia ignude e bianche.

che se giù cadono stanche
è per poco, è a breve pace.
Poi la sua bocca che tace,
tutto in lei mi dice: ancora.

Spunta in ciel la rosea aurora,
ed il sonno ella ne apporta,
che a goder ci riconforta
della grande unica cosa.

2)   Io non so più dolce cosa
dell'amore; ma più scaltro
ma di te più ardente, è un altro
che a soffrir nato mi sento.

Non la gioia ma il tormento
dell'amore è il mio diletto;
me lo tengo chiuso in petto
la sua immagine in me vario.

E cammino solitario
per i monti e per i prati,
con negli occhi imprigionati
cari volti, gesti arcani.

Sixth Fugue (Canto in 3 voices)

1)   I know no sweeter thing
than love when one is young,
than lovers gladly drunk
and dying one within the other.

I know no greater sorrow
than not to know this boon.
Her two white and naked arms
are the only chains I wear,

and if they ever drop in weariness,
it is only for a moment's rest,
and soon her silent mouth, and
all about her tells me: more.

Then in the sky the rosy dawn
appears, to bring us sleep
and comfort, that we may enjoy
that great and single thing.

2)   I know no sweeter thing
than love; and yet one shrewder
than you, more fervent as I,
feel as though born to suffer.

Not the joy, but the torment
of love is my delight;
and I keep it deep inside
and change its form within me.

I walk alone about
the hills and meadows
with cherished faces, secret
acts, imprisoned in my eyes.

Mi dilungo dagli umani:
profanar temo repente
quella ch'è nella mia mente
una tanto dolce cosa.

3)   Io non so più dolce cosa
di pensarmi. Il puro amore
di cui ardo, dal mio cuore
nasce, e tutto a lui ritorna.

Quando annotta e quando aggiorna
io mi beo d'esser me stessa.
È la cura mia indefessa
adornarmi per me sola.

La mia voce in alto vola,
scende al basso; il male e il bene
tutto è puro quando viene
all'azzurra mia pupilla,

come a un'acqua che tranquilla,
coi colori della sera,
specchia i monti, la riviera,
i viventi, ogni lor cosa.

1)   Io non so più dolce cosa
dell'ascosa mia dimora,
in cui tutto annuncia un'ora,
in cui tutto la ricorda.

Dentro come tomba è sorda,
non le giungono rumori;
vi riflettono splendori
del dì vetri pinti ad arte.

D'Oriente in lei v'è parte
per i miei lunghi riposi;
per i giochi gaudiosi
ampio ha il talamo e profondo

I keep away from other people:
I do not wish to sully
that which in my mind
is so sweet a thing.

3)   I know no sweeter thing
than to think about myself.
My pure and ardent love
is for my heart alone.

When night falls and day breaks
I rejoice in who I am.
Unceasingly I strive
to shine for me alone.

My voice soars high,
dips low; good and bad,
all turns pure within
the blue iris of my eye,

as in a placid lake
that with the evening's colors
mirrors the hills, the shore,
the people and their world.

1)   I know no sweeter thing
than my secluded home,
where all anticipates and
all recalls a single moment.

It's silent as a tomb within,
beyond the reach of sound;
through finely painted windows
shine the the splendors of the day.

There's something of the East in there,
for my long periods of rest;
and for my games of bliss
the bed is wide and deep.

Tutto il bello che nel mondo
prende e alletta gli occhi tuoi,
là raccolto veder puoi
per la grande unica cosa.

2)   Io non so più dolce cosa
dell'ascosa mia stanzetta,
sempre in vista a me diletta,
nuda come una prigione.

Poche cose vi son, buone
sol per me, per la mia vita.
I rumori della vita
giungon sì, ma di lontano.

Tutto quanto al mondo è vano,
che mal dura e mal s'innova,
spazio amico in lei ritrova
qual pulviscolo in un ciglio.

Là in un canto è il mio giaciglio,
quasi il letto d'un guerriero.
Con me giace il mio pensiero,
la mia grande unica cosa.

3)   Io non so più dolce cosa,
né dimora altra mi piace,
che vagar nella mia pace,
come nube in cielo vasto.

A me stessa, è vero, basto,
non mi punge alcuna brama;
pure amar posso chi m'ama,
e investirlo del mio fuoco.

Voi m'udite ora; fra poco
chi sarà da me beato?
Forse un misero cascato
fino al fondo giù dell'onta.

All the beauty in the world
that captivates your eyes
you will find gathered there
for that great and single thing.

2)   I know no sweeter thing
than my secluded room,
forever my two eyes' delight,
naked as a prison cell.

The few things there are good
for me alone, and for my life.
The sounds of life do reach me
there, but from afar.

All that in the world is vain
and barely lasts or ill revives,
there finds a welcome
as of dust upon an eyelash.

In one corner lies my cot,
a little like a soldier's bed.
And with me lies my thought,
my great and single thing.

3)   I know no sweeter thing,
no dwelling to my taste,
than to be at peace to wander
like a cloud in the great sky.

I am to myself enough,
it's true, am prodded by no
yearning. Beloved, though, my lover
I may love, and fire with my fire.

So hear me now: who of you
will soon know happiness by me?
A wretch, perhaps, fallen
to the very depths of shame?

Una grazia piena e pronta
gli fa impeto nel cuore;
trasfigura il suo dolore
nella grande unica cosa.

1)   Io non so più dolce cosa
dell'amore in giovanezza;
pur v'ha, dicono, un'ebbrezza
che sta sopra anche di quella.

Non per me che in una bella
forma appago ogni desio,
ma per chi si sente a un dio
nel volere assomigliante.

Non fanciulla, non amante
—vivo rappolo autunnale—
la dolcezza per lui vale
di piegarti al suo destino.

E si taglia egli un cammino
tra gli ignavi e tra gli ostili.
Pei tuoi sogni giovanili
o non so più grande cosa.

2)   Io non so più grande cosa
di chi, al cenno altrui soggetto,
sente d'essere un eletto
all'interna libertà.

E non ha felicità
che non venga a lui da questo.
Non t'inganni il suo esser mesto,
il suo aspetto non t'inganni.

Fra i tormenti, negli affanni
propri solo alla sua sorte,
solo a lui s'apron le porte
d'un occulto paradiso.

A full and ready grace
would give his heart a boost,
transform his sorrow into
that great and single thing.

1)   I know no sweeter thing
than love when one is young;
and yet, they say, an even
greater ecstasy exists.

Not for me, who in the beauty
of a figure slake all my desire,
but for one who in his will
can feel as like a god.

For him the sweetness lies
in no young girl or lover
— bright grapes of autumn—
but in making his fate yours.
And he beats himself a path
among the indolent and hostile.
For your youthful dreams
I know no greater thing.

2)   I know no greater thing
than one who, subject to
another's whim, feels blessed
with inner freedom

and knows no happiness
that does not spring from this.
Let not his somber mood
or gloomy mien deceive you.

Amid the torments and troubles
proper to his fate alone,
a secret heaven's gates
open up to him alone.

Là uccisor non v'è, né ucciso,
e non torbida demenza.
Dalla mesta adolescenza
io non so più lieta cosa.

3)   Io non so più lieta cosa
del sereno in cui mi godo.
Pure quando parlar v'odo,
e parlando vaneggiare,

la mia pace vorrei dare
per la vostra, oh lo potessi!
Ma dai limiti concessi
non c'è dato, o cari, uscire.

Folle amore, orgoglio d'ire,
paradiso me non tocca.
Se baciarmi sulla bocca
fosse lecito a un mortale,

proverebbe un senso, quale
della morte è forse il gelo:
tanto azzurro è in me di cielo,
tanto in me brucia l'amore.

1)   Io non so più caldo amore
dell'amor di questa terra,
quando tutta al cor la serra
nell'abbraccio il suo fedele.

Come pomo sa di miele
e d'acerbo al mio palato;
se un amaro v'è mischiato
è perché mai me ne sazi.

Se i tormenti, se gli strazi
che tu esalti, mi prepara,
quale ho mai cosa più cara
della sola che possiedo

No killer there, nor victim,
nor riotous dementia.
In gloomy adolescence
I know no brighter thing.

3)   I know no brighter thing
than the calm in which I bask.
Even as I hear you speak,
and while speaking start to rave,

oh how I wish I could
make my peace your own!
But outside given limits
we are fated not to go.

Foolish love and wrathful pride
don't reach me in my paradise.
If mortal man were granted leave
to kiss me on the lips,

he would feel something like,
perhaps, the chill of death:
as much blue of sky as shines in me,
so burns love's fire equally.

1)   I know no warmer love
than love for this our earth,
as when her faithful devotee
enfolds her all in one embrace.

And just as fruit may taste
of honey or tart to my tongue,
if bitterness there be, it is
that I never have enough of it.

If the torment and the pain
you glorify await me,
what do I have more precious
than my one and only thing?

Ma mi guardo intorno, e vedo
altro ancor che strazio e lutto
sulla terra, dove al frutto
morde ognun del caldo amore.

2)   Io non so più cieco amore
dell'amore della vita.
Nella mia stanza romita;
passeggiando solitario;

da un delirio unico e vario
tutta notte posseduto,
quante, quante volte ho avuto
il pensiero io di lasciarla!

Te felice se puoi darla
del tuo amor nei rischi avvolto;
più felice ancora, e molto,
chi a gettarla si fa un vanto;

chi la getta come un guanto
al destino che disprezza.
Ah, perché la giovanezza
della morte ha in sé l'amore?

3)   Io non so di questo amore,
io non so di questa morte:
immutabile è la sorte
conceduta alla mia gioia.

Ch'altri viva, ch'altri muoia
il pensiero in me non nacque.
A crearmi si compiacque
forse un'anima in un sogno.

Forse un'anima in un sogno
così bella mi creava,
con la mente al bene schiava,
con l'azzurra mia pupilla,

Yet if I look around, I see
far more than pain and sorrow
on this earth, where each
may bite of love's warm fruit.

2) I know no blinder love
than our great love of life.
When in my lonely room,
or walking by myself,

when haunted through the night
by one same, changing madness,
how often have I contemplated
leaving it forever!

Happy he who gives his life
surrounded by love's dangers.
More happy still, by much,
he that proudly throws it down

like a gauntlet, before
his flouted destiny.
Ah, why does youth
have such a love of death?

3) I know not of this love,
I know not of this death;
the fate my joy is granted
is eternal, never changing.

The lives and deaths of others
enter not into my thoughts.
I must have been created
by a soul within a dream.

A soul within a dream, perhaps,
fashioned me so beautiful,
with a mind enthralled to goodness
the blue iris of my eye

come un'acqua che tranquilla
tutto specchia e nulla offende.
Ah, perché tra voi mi prende
desiderio d'altra cosa?

1)   Io non so più dolce cosa
del presente. Ai dì remoti
mi smarrivo anch'io in ignoti
desideri, ora non più.

Voglio il bene, e nulla più
di cui possa uomo godere.
Belle forme amo vedere,
possederle amo più ancora.

La bellezza m'innamora,
e la grazia m'incatena;
e non sogno un'altra pena,
se non è di ciò l'assenza.

Alla mesta adolescenza
ho lasciato i sogni vani.
Esser uomo tra gli umani,
io non so più dolce cosa.

2)   Io non so più dolce cosa,
né più amara a chi n'è privo.
Nel presente appena vivo,
vedo più ch'altri non vede.

Beni a cui nessuno crede
mi sorridono al pensiero.
Tutto il mondo un cimitero,
senza quelli mi diventa.

Tutta in me la gioia è spenta,
sana gioia in cui t'esalti.
Troppo bassi son, tropp'alti
forse i sogni che altrui taccio?

that like a placid lake
mirrors all and offends none.
Ah, why among you two
do I wish for something else?

1)   I know no sweeter thing
than now. In days long past
I too would lose myself
in vague desires. No more.

Now I only want the goodness
man may best enjoy.
It's lovely forms I love to see,
and to possess, still better yet.

Beauty makes me fall in love,
grace holds me in its chains;
and I feel no other pain than this,
except when this is lacking.

I have left my useless dreams
to gloomy adolescence.
To be a man among humanity,
I know no sweeter thing.

2)   I know no sweeter thing,
or for those without, more bitter.
Barely living in the present,
I see more than others see.

Good things no one believes in
smile at me in my mind.
For me the world becomes
a graveyard in their absence.

All joy in me dies out,
the pure joy you exult in.
Are the dreams I keep from others
too base, perhaps, too lofty?

Ahi, sognando io mi disfaccio;
notti ho insonni e giorno vani.
Esser uomo tra gli umani,
no, non v'è più dolce cosa.

3)   Io non so più dolce cosa
che potermi in voi mutare,
solo un'ora; ma tornare
potrei dopo alla mia pace?

Sarei dopo ancor capace
di adomarmi per me sola?
La delizia che s'invola
chi sa mai se si riacquista?

Io che vedo e non son vista,
se soffrir potessi il morso
della brama, forse il corso
qui più a lungo avrei fermato.

Forse avrebbe uno ascoltato
sul mio labbro accenti vani:
ch'esser uomo tra gli umani
parve a me una dolce cosa.

1)   Io non so più dolce cosa
della dolce giovanezza.
Fino il vento l'accarezza
sulla gota, o poco punge.

Se la gloria a lei s'aggiunge
sommo è il bene che in te rechi.
A me basta udirne gli echi,
berne a lungo le parole.

Giovanezza in me si duole
solo d'esser fuggitiva.
Altra pena non ho viva,
fuori questa, nel mio cuore.

Alas, in dreaming I'm undone!
I have sleepless nights and useless days!
Yes, to be a man among humanity,
there is no sweeter thing.

3)   I know no sweeter thing
than the chance to become you,
just for an hour; but after,
would I find my peace again?

Would I again be able
to shine for me alone?
Who knows whether bliss, once gone,
can ever be had again?

I who see and am not seen,
if I could feel desire's bite,
perhaps I sooner would have stopped
the course of our exchange.

Perhaps somebody would have heard
vain words upon my lips,
that to be a man among humanity
seemed to me the sweetest thing.

1)   I know no sweeter thing
than our own sweet youth.
Its cheek the gentle wind
caresses, or seldom stings.

If to youth you add renown,
you will possess the greatest good.
I am happy just to hear
its echoes, drink deep its words.

Youth to me is painful
only in its fleetingness.
No other keen affliction
grieves my heart but this.

E obliarla dell'amore
anche appresi nell'incanto.
Rattristare in te di pianto
come puoi sì breve cosa?

2)   Io non so più breve cosa
della dolce giovanezza.
Di me forse più l'apprezza
chi è già giunto alla sua sera.

Della gloria menzognera
non ascolto io la lusinga.
Bella ogni altro se la finga,
io il suo fascino ho in me estinto.

Amo sol chi in ceppi avvinto,
nell'orror d'una segreta,
può aver l'anima più lieta
di chi a sangue lo percuote.

Bagna il pianto le sue gote,
cresce in cor la strana ebbrezza.
Per lui prova giovanezza
la sua grazia anche ai supplizi.

3)   Non mi nego ai tuoi supplizi,
non ho in odio i tuoi piaceri;
non so come, i miei pensieri
si smarriscono nei vostri.

Per la fede che mi mostri,
tu a una gioia, e tu a un dolore,
se mortal fosse il mio cuore
di lui quanto vorrei darvi!

Pur son lieta di mirarvi,
e l'udirvi anche m'è caro.
Per voi provo un dono raro,
del diamante la virtù;

Yet in love's spell I've even
learned to disregard this.
How can you be saddened
by a thing so very brief?

2)   I know no briefer thing
than our own sweet youth.
Perhaps those in their twilight
better cherish it than I.

Renown's mendacious flatteries
I do not even hear.
Let others paint her beautiful,
her charms sway me no more.

I love only him who,
though fettered in a horrid cell,
can have a lighter spirit
than the one who beats him bloody.

As tears stream down his cheek,
a strange elation moves him.
His grace reveals a youthfulness,
even under torture.

3)   I don't deny your torture,
nor do I spurn your pleasure;
my thoughts, I don't know how,
get lost among your own.

Such faith you show me each,
one in joy and one in sorrow,
that if my heart were mortal,
so much of it I'd give you both!

Still I'm happy just to gaze at you,
to hear you speak as well.
A rare gift you bring out in me:
the virtue of a diamond that,

che in bei gialli, in rossi, in blu,
quando a un raggio di sol brilla,
lo splendor nativo immilla;
e non so più dolce cosa.

1)   Io non so più dolce cosa
di ascoltarti, chiara voce.
Ma se nulla a te non nuoce,
ecco, esaudi quanto chiedo.

Te che ascolto e che non vedo
sei, celata, una fanciulla?
Se tal sei, dalla tua culla
d'aria scendi al mio richiamo.

La tua faccia veder bramo,
senza lei m'è il giorno oscuro.
Tanto bella io ti figuro
come dolce a udirti sei.

La tua bocca io bacerei,
tenerezza che tu ignori.
Uno fare di due ardori,
io non so più dolce cosa.

2)   Io non so più dolce cosa,
né più vana, amico errante.
Parla un angelo, e un amante
in lui pinge il tuo desio.

Oh t'inchina invece al mio,
che di solo udirti ho sete.
D'onde vieni, a quali mète
sei rivolta, io dir ti prego.

All'abbraccio te non lego
d'un mortale, aereo fuoco.
Ma dimora ancora un poco
qui con noi, fra terra e cielo

when brightened by a ray of sun,
in lovely yellows, reds and blues
increases endlessly its inborn splendor;
I know no sweeter thing.

1)   I know no sweeter thing
than the sound of your clear voice.
But if it costs you nothing,
please grant me what I ask.

You, whom I hear but do not see,
are you a young girl, hiding?
If so, then come down from
your bed of air to me.

I long to see your face,
the day is dark without it.
How lovely it must be I know,
so sweet is it to hear you.

I want to kiss your mouth,
you've never known that tenderness.
To make two passions one:
I know no sweeter thing.

2)   I know no sweeter thing,
nor one more vain, mistaken friend.
Here speaks an angel, while your
desire makes of him a lover.

Oh yield instead to mine,
for I only yearn to hear you.
Tell me, please, whence you've come,
and what your purposes may be.

Airy fire, yours is not,
I think, a mortal's embrace.
But stay a while yet with us,
between the earth and sky.

Forse invan mirarti anelo?
Non hai corpo, non hai viso;
non sei forse che un sorriso.
Parla amica, oh parla ancora!

3)   Parla tu, gentile, ancora,
se di udirmi ancora agogni.
Non m'hai forse nei tuoi sogni
prima d'ora mai raggiunta?

Quando in ciel l'aurora spunta?
Nella veglia che beata
chiama questi, e n'ha celata
la sua nausea egli, il disgusto.

Nata son dal suo disgusto,
nata son dal tuo tormento:
tanto viva esser mi sento
quanto amate il viver mio.

Ma se voi tacete, anch'io,
ecco, in aere mi risolvo;
con voi libera m'evolvo,
muoio libera con voi.

Perhaps in vain I long to see you?
Without body, without face,
perhaps you're no more than a smile.
Speak more, dear friend, oh speak!

3)   You, good friend, must speak more
if you wish to hear me still.
Have you not perhaps in dreams
already come to me before?

As when the dawn appears?
—in nightlong vigils he calls
blest, yet hides the malaise,
the disgust they cause in him . . .

Of that disgust I am born.
Of that torment I am born.
I feel only as alive
as you can love my living.

Yet if you should fall silent,
I shall dissolve in air.
Free I come to life through you,
and through you I die free.

Congedo

Dalla marea che un popolo ha sommerso,
e me con esso, ancora
levo la testa? Ancora
ascolto? Ancora non è tutto perso?

Envoi

From the tide that has engulfed a people,
and me with them, do I still
raise my head? Do I still
listen? Is all not yet lost?

from

IL PICCOLO BERTO

LITTLE BERTO

(1929-31)

Tre poesie alla mia balia

1

Mia figlia
mi tiene il braccio intorno al collo, ignudo;
ed io alia sua carezza m'addormento.

Divento
legno in mare caduto che sull'onda
galleggia. E dove alla vicina sponda
anelo, il flutto mi porta lontano.
Oh, come sento che lottare è vano!
Oh, come in petto per dolcezza il cuore
vien meno!

Al seno
approdo di colei che Berto ancora
mi chiama, al primo, all'amoroso seno,
ai verdi paradisi dell'infanzia.

Three Poems to my Wet-Nurse

1

My daughter
wraps her small arm round my naked neck.
I fall asleep to her caress

and turn into
a piece of driftwood floating on the waves,
yearning for the nearby shore but carried
by the current far to sea.
Ah, how vain it feels to struggle!
Ah, how tenderly my heart within me
falters!

I fall to land
upon the breast of her for whom I still am
Berto, upon that first and loving breast,
green paradise of childhood.

2

Insonne
mi levo all'alba. Che farà la mia
vecchia nutrice? Posso forse ancora
là ritrovarla, nel suo negozietto?
Come vive, se vive? E a lei m'affretto,
pure una volta, con il cuore ansante,

Eccola: è viva; in piedi dopo tante
vicende e tante stagioni. Un sorriso
illumina, a vedermi, il volto ancora
bello per me, misterioso. È l'ora
a lei d'aprire. Ad aiutarla accorso
scalzo fanciullo, del nativo colle
tutto improntato, la persona china
leggera, ed alza la saracinesca.

Nella rosata in cielo e in terra fresca
mattina io ben la ritrovavo. E sono
a lei d'allora. Quel fanciullo io sono
che a lei spontaneo soccorreva; immagine
di me, d'uno di me perduto . . .

2

At first light
I get up from a sleepless night. I wonder
what my old nurse is up to? If I went back now,
to her little store, would I still find her there?
How does she live, if she lives at all? And so I
rush off one more time to her, heart racing.

There she is: alive, still standing after all those
trials, all those seasons. At the sight of me
a smile brightens her face, still lovely as ever
to me, still mysterious. It is time for her
to open up. To her aid a barefoot boy
comes runnng, the very image of his
native hill; he bends his nimble body
forward, raising up the rolling gate.

On a morning tinted rose across the land
and sky, I've found her yet again. And
I am hers again. I am that boy who ran
instinctively to her assistance, that mirror
of myself, of someone now lost to me . . .

3

                                        . . . Un grido
s'alza di bimbo sulle scale. E piange
anche la donna che va via. Si frange
per sempre un cuore in quel momento.

                              Adesso
sono passati quarant'anni.
                        Il bimbo
è un uomo adesso, quasi un vecchio, esperto
di molti beni e molti mali. È Umberto
Saba quel bimbo. E va, di pace in cerca,
a conversare colla sua nutrice;
che anch'ella fu di lasciarlo infelice,
non volontaria lo lasciava. Il mondo
fu a lui sospetto d'allora, fu sempre
(o tale almeno gli parve) nemico.

Appeso al muro è un orologio antico
così che manda un suono quasi morto.
Lo regolava nel tempo felice
il dolce balio; è un caro a lui conforto
regolarlo in suo luogo. Anche gli piace
a sera accendere il lume, restare
da lei gli piace, fin ch'ella gli,,dice:

"È tardi. Torna da tua moglie, Berto."

3

                       . . . A child's cry
rings out in the stairwell. A woman, leaving,
also weeps. And in that moment someone's
heart is broken for all time.

                               Forty years
have passed since then.
                  The child
is now a man, almost an old man, and versed
in many things, both good and bad. That child
is Umberto Saba. And, in search of peace
of mind, he's gone to talk with his wet-nurse.
She too, on leaving him, felt bad or worse
than he, and did not leave him voluntarily.
Since that day the world to him has been
uncertain, always (so it seems) against him.

On the wall there hangs a clock so old
its chimes sound almost dead.
In happier days the nurse's gentle husband
used to set it right. Now Berto, in his stead,
takes sweet comfort fixing it himself. Round
nightfall he also takes pleasure lighting the lamp
and lingering a long time, until she says:

"It's late now, Berto. Go home to your wife."

Cucina economica

Immensa gratitudine alla vita
che ha conservate queste care cose;
oceano di delizie, anima mia!

Oh come tutto al suo posto si trova!
Oh come tutto al suo posto è restato!
In grande povertà anche è salvezza.
Della gialla polenta la bellezza
mi commuove per gli ocche; il cuore sale,
per fascini più occulti, ad un estremo
dell'umano possible sentire.
Io, se potessi, io qui vorrei morire,
qui mi trasse un istinto. Indifferenti
cenano accanto a me due muratori;
e un vecchietto che il pasto senza vino
ha consumato, in sé si è chiuso e al caldo
dolce accogliente, come nascituro
dentro il grembo materno. Egli assomiglia
forse al mio povero padre ramingo,
cui malediva mia madre; un bambino
esterrefatto ascoltava. Vicino
mi sento alle mie origini; mi sento,
se non erro, ad un mio luogo tornato;

al popolo in cui muoio, onde son nato.

Bargain Kitchen

My boundless thanks to life
for preserving these beloved things,
ocean of pleasures, my soul!

Look how everything is in its place!
Look how everything has stayed in place!
In great poverty also lies salvation.
By the power of sight I am touched
by the beautiful yellow polenta; by virtue
of more hidden charms my heart soars
to an extreme of possible human feeling.
I would die here if I could,
drawn to this place by instinct. Beside me
two stonemasons dine indifferently;
an old man has eaten his meal
without wine, withdrawn into himself and
the sweet warmth arising as if
from a mother's womb. He looks
a little like my poor vagabond father,
whom my mother used to curse, while
a little boy listened in horror. I feel
close to my beginnings; I feel I have returned
—unless I am mistaken—to a place of my own:

to the people of my dying, the people of my birth.

Partenza e ritorno

Di padre
serbo in Serbia era nata. E aveva a Padova
la bella casa signorile.
                              Disse
mia madre un giorno: "Se mandassi Umberto
da zia Stellina e dall'Elvira? Forse
al suo ritorno alfine m'amerà.
Forse, lontano restando, la Peppa,
l'eterna Peppa dimenticherà."

E andai lontano, a Padova. L'Elvira molto
mi piacque, meno assai la zia,
vecchia donna e severa. E quante cose
la bella Elvira m'apprese! le lettere
dell'alfabeto, un po' d'astronomia
perfino. Il nome di lei mi piaceva,
e la sua stanza, e il suo profumo ch'era
di rose e mandorle amare. E una sera,
dalla finestra che dà sul giardino,
sento per nome chiamarmi. "Mi pare
—dico—mi pare di sentir la voce
della mia mamma di Trieste."

                                        Un muro
vedo ed ombre danzanti, un'altra ombra
china su me, che mi tranquilla. Sono
ritornato a Trieste; in un lettuccio
giaccio ammalato. Ma, guarito appena,
chiedo ancora di lei, della mia amica.
E tanto faccio che le son condotto,
subito. più non m'aspettava, io credo,
la mia buona, la mia fida nutrice.

"Oh Berto, oh Berto!" esclamava, felice
a me versando il caffelatte. Io tutti
i miei progressi le appresi. Poi quando
—come un secreto fra noi due—mi chiese
se stavo bene a Padova, se stavo

Departure and Return

She was born
in Serbia, of a Serbian father. And she lived in Padua,
in a beautiful house.
                         One day
my mother said: "And what if I sent Umberto
to stay with Aunt Stellina and Elvira? Maybe
at last he'll love me when he returns.
Maybe, being so far away, he'll finally
forget Peppa, the eternal Peppa."

And so I was sent far away, to Padua. Elvira
I liked very much, my old aunt much less.
She was too severe. But how many things
the pretty Elvira taught me! The letters
of the alphabet, even a bit of
astronomy. I liked her name, her room,
the smell of her perfume, a scent
of rose and bitter almond. Then one evening,
from the window that looked onto the garden,
I heard someone call me by name. "That sounds
like mama's voice," I said, "that's
my mama from Trieste."

                                    I see
a wall and dancing shadows, another
shadow leaning over me, to comfort me. I am
back in Trieste, lying sick in bed.
But as soon as I'm a little better,
I ask for her, my friend, immediately.
And I make such a fuss that I'm taken
to her at once. My dear and faithful wet-nurse,
I think, had given up waiting for me.

"Oh Berto, Berto!" she cried out for joy,
pouring me coffee-and-milk. I told her
all that I had learned. And when she asked me—
as a secret just between us two—if I was
happy down in Padua, if I preferred to be

meglio laggiù o con mia madre: "Era bello
coll'Elvira—le dissi;—ma con te
—e la pregai si abbassasse, che dirle
io volli questo in un orecchio—è ancora
più bello."

       Alla sua cara Itaca Ulisse
non ebbe forse un più lieto ritorno
del mio, di Berto in via del Monte. Il giorno
era sereno fulgido; modello
rimasto in me d'ogni bel giorno, immagine
viva parlante di felicità.

down there or with my mother, I said:
"It was good with Elvira, but with you,"
and I asked her to bend down, because I
wished to whisper in her ear, "it's so
much better."

        To his beloved Ithaca Odysseus
returned perhaps no happier than I,
Berto, returned to Via del Monte.
The day was clear and bright, and became
for me the model of every beautiful day,
the living, speaking image of happiness.

VOLUME III

(1933-1954)

from

PAROLE

WORDS

(1933-34)

Risveglio

La notte vede più del giorno.

$\qquad\qquad\qquad$ Parte
di quella ancora, ad occhi aperti sono
il montone dipinto da Bolaffio,
che solo torce di tra il branco il muso
umano.

Non vano
godimento ne provo; quasi vivo
fosse l'amico che pur ieri è morto.

Waking Up

The night sees more than the day.
Still
half-dreaming, in my open eyes I am
the ram Bolaffio painted,
who alone among the flock
twists his human muzzle.

No vain
amusement, this. It's as if
my friend, dead yesterday, were alive.

Neve

Neve che turbini in alto ed avvolgi
le cose di tacito manto,
una creatura di pianto
vedo per te sorridere; un baleno
d'allegrezza che il mesto viso illumini,
e agli occhi miei come un tesoro scopri.

Neve che cadi dall'alto e noi copri,
coprici ancora, all'infinito. Imbianca
la città con le case e con le chiese,
il porto con le navi; le distese
dei prati, i mari agghiaccia; della terra
fa'—tu augusta e pudica—un astro spento,
una gran pace di morte. E che tale
essa rimanga un tempo interminato,
un lungo volger d'evi.
                          Il risveglio,
pensa il risveglio, noi due soli, in tanto
squallore.
              In cielo
gli angeli con le trombe, in cuore acute
dilaceranti nostalgie, ridesti
vaghi ricordi, e piangere d'amore.

Snow

Snow in whirlwinds overhead,
wrapping the world in a soundless mantle,
I see a creature of sorrow
smile at you, a flash
of joy light up a sad face.
You unveil treasures before my eyes.

Snow from above that covers us all,
cover us more and forever. Whiten
the city with its houses and churches,
the port with its ships; freeze the wide-open
fields and seas; in your majesty
and modesty make a spent star of this earth,
grant her the silence of death. And let her
thus remain for a time without end,
a long passing of ages.
                        The reawakening,
just think, the two of us, alone, amid such
desolation.
            The angels
with their trumpets in heaven, the sharp
and bitter yearning in my heart, you stir
vague memories, and cries for love.

Ceneri

Ceneri
di cose morte, di mali perduti,
di contatti ineffabfli, di muti
sospiri;

vivide
fiamme da voi m'investono nell'atto
che d'ansia in ansia approssimo alle soglie
del sonno;

e al sonno,
con quei legami appassionati e teneri
ch'ànno il bimbo e la madre, ed a voi ceneri
mi fondo.

L'angoscia
insidia al varco, io la disarmo. Come
un beato la via del paradiso,
salgo una scala, sosto ad una porta
a cui suonavo in altri tempi. Il tempo
ha ceduto di colpo.
                    Mi sento,
con i panni e con l'anima di allora,
in una luce di folgore; al cuore
una gioia si abbatte vorticosa
come la fine.
                    Ma non grido.
                              Muto
parto dell'ombre per l'immenso impero.

Ashes

Ashes
of dead things, troubles forgotten,
ineffable contacts, voiceless
sighs;

from you
bright flames rise to envelop me,
as from worry to worry I near the threshold
of sleep;

and into sleep,
as child into mother's arms in tenderness
and love, into those ashes
I melt.

Anguish
threatens the crossing, but I disarm it. Like
a blessèd on the way to heaven,
I climb a staircase, stop before a door
whose doorbell I once used to ring. Time
suddenly vanishes.
      Wearing
my old clothes and the self I once was,
I am bathed in radiant light; the joy
in my heart founders, whirls
like death itself.
      But I do not cry out.
         Silent
I leave for the shadows' vast realm.

Primavera

Primavera che a me non piaci, io voglio
dire di te che di una strada l'angolo
svoltando, il tuo presagio mi feriva
come una lama. L'ombra ancor sottile
di nudi rami sulla terra ancora
nuda mi turba, quasi anch'io potessi
dovessi
rinascere. La tomba
sembra insicura al tuo appressarsi, antica
primavera, che più d'ogni stagione
crudelmente risusciti ed uccidi.

Spring

I don't care for you at all. It used to be
that when I turned a corner in the street,
the premonition of your coming would cut me
like a razor. The still slender shadows
of bare branches cast upon the still bare earth
make me uneasy, as if I too
might somehow be
reborn. Ancient
spring, even the grave seems uncertain
at your approach. You of all the seasons
most cruelly resurrect and kill.

Confine

Parla a lungo con me la mia compagna
di cose tristi, gravi, che sul cuore
pesano come una pietra; viluppo
di mali inestricabile, che alcuna
mano, e la mia, non può sciogliere.
                                        Un passero
della casa di faccia sulla gronda
posa un attimo, al sol brilla, ritorna
al cielo azzurro che gli è sopra.
                                        O lui
tra i beati beato! Ha l'ali, ignora
la mia pena secreta, il mio dolore
d'uomo giunto a un confine: alla certezza
di non poter soccorrere chi s'ama.

Limit

On and on my woman speaks to me
of grave and somber things that weigh upon
the heart like a rock, indissoluble
tangle of troubles that no hand,
not mine, could unravel.
                              A sparrow
lands a moment on the eave of the house
before us, shining in the sun, then
returns to the blue sky above him.
                              O blessed
among the blessed, that one! He can fly, knows
nothing of my secret sorrow, the pain of a man
who has reached a limit: the knowledge
he is powerless to help the one he loves.

Ulisse

O tu che sei sì triste ed hai presagi
d'orrore—Ulisse al declino—nessuna
dentro l'anima tua dolcezza aduna
la Brama
per una
pallida sognatrice di naufragi
che t'ama?

Ulysses

O sad Ulysses in decline, seer
of terrible omens, does
no sweetness in your soul foment
Desire
for a
pale dreamer of shipwrecks
who loves you?

Tredicesima partita

Sui gradini un manipolo sparuto
si riscaldava di se stesso.

                  E quando
—smisurata raggiera—il sole spense
dietro una casa il suo barbaglio, il campo
schiarì il presentimento della notte.
Correvano su e giù le maglie rosse,
le maglie bianche, in una luce d'una
strana iridata transparenza. Il vento
deviava il pallone, la Fortuna
si rimetteva agli occhi la benda.

Piaceva
essere così pochi intirizziti
uniti,
come ultima uomini su un monte,
a guardare di là l'ultima gara.

Thirteenth Match

On the steps a meager crowd
tried to keep themselves warm.
                              And when
the sun's glare—boundless radiance—
died behind a house, the action on the field
lightened the gloom of the coming night.
Red jerseys and white jerseys ran
back and forth, in a strange transparent
iridescence. The wind diverted the ball
from its course, while Lady Luck
put the blindfold back over her eyes.

It was good
to be so small a gathering,
frozen stiff
together
like the last men on a hill
watching the very last game.

Cuore

Cuore serrato come in una morsa,
    mio triste cuore,
rallegrati di questa ultima corsa
    contro il dolore.

Quale angoscia non hai viva abbracciata,
    vivo restando?
Una piccola cosa ti è bastata,
    di quando in quando.

Heart

Heart squeezed as in a vice,
       sad heart of mine,
rejoice at this one final race
       against the pain.

What living anguish have you not embraced,
       while living still?
Some little thing for you sufficed,
       from time to time.

Inverno

È notte, inverno rovinoso. Un poco
sollevi le tendine, e guardi. Vibrano
i tuoi capelli selvaggi, la gioia
ti dilata improvvisa l'occhio nero;
che quello che hai veduto—era un'immagine
della fine del mondo—ti conforta
l'intimo cuore, lo fa caldo e pago.

Un uomo si avventura per un lago
di ghiaccio, sotto una lampada storta.

Winter

It is night, raging winter. You lift
the curtain slightly, look outside. Your
wild hair trembles, a sudden joy
opens your dark eyes wide:
for what you've just seen—an image
of the world's end—consoles you deep inside
your heart, makes you feel warm and satisfied.

A man ventures out on a lake
of ice, under a crooked lamppost.

Poesia

È come a un uomo battuto dal vento,
accecato di neve—intorno pinge
un inferno polare la città –
l'aprirsi, lungo il muro, di una porta.

Entra. Ritrova la bontà non morta,
la dolcezza di un caldo angolo. Un nome
posa dimenticato, un bacio sopra
ilari volti che più non vedeva
che oscuri in sogni minacciosa.
                                    Torna
egli alla strada, anche la strada è un'altra.
Il tempo al bello si è rimesso, i ghiacci
spezzano mani operose, il celeste
rispunta in cielo e nel suo cuore. E pensa
che ogni estremo di mali un bene annunci.

Poem

It is like the opening, to a wind-
battered man—blinded by the snow
that all around him paints the town
a polar hell—of a door along a wall.

He enters. There he finds goodness still alive
and the comfort of a warm corner.
A name falls forgotten, a kiss, on
laughing faces he's not seen for ages
except in shadows in his nightmares.
                       When he goes
back in the street, it too has changed.
The weather has cleared up, busy hands
are breaking ice, the blue sky
reappears above and in his heart. And he thinks
the worst things always herald something good.

Felicità

La giovanezza cupida di pesi
porge spontenea al carico le spalle.
Non regge. Piange di malinconia.

Vagabondaggio, evasione, poesia
cari prodigi sul tardi! Sul tardi
l'aria si affina ed i passi si fanno
leggeri.
Oggi è il meglio di ieri,
se non è ancora la felicità.

Assumeremo un giorno la bontà
del suo volto, vedremo alcuno sciogliere
come un fumo il suo inutile dolore.

Happiness

Youth, in its gravity, is forever
eager to take a burden on its shoulders.
But it cannot bear the load, and cries in bitterness.

Drifting, distraction, poetry,
precious wonders late in the day! Late in the day
the air grows thin, one walks
with lighter step.
Today is the best of yesterday,
even if it's still not happiness.

One day its good face shall be ours
to wear, someone shall come and blow
away like smoke its needless sorrow.

Tre città

1   MILANO

Fra le tue pietre e le tue nebbie faccio
villeggiatura. Mi riposo in Piazza
del Duomo. Invece
di stelle
ogni sera si accendono parole.

Nulla riposa della vita come
la vita.

Three Cities

Among your stones and fog I am
on holiday. I rest in Piazza
del Duomo. Every evening
words
—not stars—light the sky.

No rest in life
like life itself.

2 TORINO

Ritornerò dentro la cerchia amabile
dei tuoi monti, alle vie che si prolungano
come squilli. Poi tosto in uno strano
silenzio fuggirò ritrovi, amici.
Ma cercherò il soldato Salamano,
il più duro a parole, il più al dovere
fermo, che in sé la tua virtú rispecchia.

Cercherò l'officina ov'egli invecchia.

2 TURIN

I shall re-enter your gentle circle
of mountains, to streets that run on
like chimes. Then, in the strange and sudden
silence, I shall avoid old haunts and friends.
But I will seek out the solider Salamano,
the toughest talker and most diligent
of all, mirror of his city's strength.

I shall find him in his workshop, growing old.

3 FIRENZE

Per abbracciare il poeta Montale
—generosa è la sua tristezza—sono
nella città che mi fu cara. È come
se ogni pietra che il piede batte fosse
il mio cuore, il mio male
di un tempo. Ma non ho rimpianti. Nasce
—altra costellazione—un'altra età.

3 FLORENCE

To embrace the poet Montale
—his is a generous gloom—I've come
to a city I once loved. Every
stone I walk on feels as if it were
my heart, my past
unhappiness. But I have no regrets.
Another constellation is rising.
Another age is born.

Sobborgo

Vecchio sobborgo improvvisato e squallido,
già campagna sassosa, poi conquista.

Sul tetto di una casa cresce l'erba,
come sui resti di un incendio. Pochi
passi più in là c'è il Pastificio, il rosso
suo fumaiolo. Ma la giostra suona
all'ultima miseria delle cose,
alle merci che sembrano rifiuti,
alle facciate delle case invase
di una lebbra che ieri era colore,
e rallegrava lontano la vista.

Come diverso il giovane barista,
pure nato di te, da te si sente!
Mi fa un caffè come un trionfo, e i buoni
occhi in volto gli ridono sportivi.

Suburb

Old suburb, slapdash and squalid,
once rocky terrain, then conquered.

Grass grows from a house's roof
and on some burnt-out ruins. A little
further on there is a Pasta factory
with a red smokestack. The carousel
plays a tune to utter wretchedness,
to merchandise that looks like trash,
to façades of houses infiltrated
by a leprosy that once was color
and made a pleasant sight from afar.

How different the young barman feels from you,
though born of your world!
He makes me a coffee in triumph,
a playful sparkle in his gentle eyes.

"Frutta erbaggi"

Erbe, frutta, colori della bella
stagione. Poche ceste ove alla sete
si rivelano dolci polpe crude.

Entra un fanciullo colle gambe nude,
imperioso, fugge via.
                     S'oscura
l'umile botteguccia, invecchia come
una madre.
              Di fuori egli nel sole
si allontana, con l'ombra sua, leggero.

"Greengrocer"

Greens, fruit, colors of the bright
season. A few baskets, to thirsty eyes
reveal sweet, raw pulp.

A barelegged boy appears,
imperious, then rushes away.
                           The humble
shop darkens, grows old
like a mother.
                    Outside, in sunlight,
he runs off, softly, with his shadow.

Donna

Quand'eri
giovinetta pungevi
come una mora di macchia. Anche il piede
t'era un'arma, o selvaggia.

Eri difficile a prendere.
                        Ancora
giovane, ancora
sei bella. I segni
degli anni, quelli del dolore, legano
l'anime nostre, una ne fanno. E dietro
i capelli nerissimi che avvolgo
alle mie dita, più non temo il piccolo
bianco puntuto orecchio demoniaco.

Woman

When just a girl
you used to sting
like a bramble bush. Even your foot
was a weapon, my wild one.

You were hard to catch.
                           Still
young you are, still
beautiful. The scars
of time and sorrow bind our souls,
of two make one. And behind
the coal-black hair I wrap around
my fingers, I no longer fear
the small white pointed devil's ear.

from

ULTIME COSE

LAST THINGS

(1935-1943)

Lavoro

Un tempo
la mia vita era facile. La terra
mi dava fiori frutta in abbondanza.

Or dissodo un terreno secco e duro.
La vanga
urta in pietre, in sterpaglia. Scavar devo
profondo, come chi cerca un tesoro.

Labor

Once
my life was easy. The earth
bore fruits and flowers in abundance.

Now I till a hard, dry land.
The spade
strikes rocks and brushwood. I must dig
deep, like someone searching for a treasure.

Violino

Avuto
di variopinti francobolli in cambio
e muto
da tanto, così dolci argentei suoni
dal tuo legno cavavo io questa notte,

mio violino, sostegno
della difficile età, di lei nato
miraggio, a oscure inquietudini porto,
che il mio dono non eri.
                      A te nei sogni
revivo, a quando a quando, di una notte.

Violin

Acquired
for some multicolored postage stamps,
retired
long ago to silence, you let your wood
bring sweet sounds to my sleep last night,

my violin, nurture
of my hardest years, mirage
born of that age, haven for dark apprehensions.
My gift you were not.
                    To you I return
to life, now and then, in the dreams of a night.

Ecco, adesso tu sai

Ecco, adesso tu sai che tra i beati
non è dimora per noi. Che la vita,
come un avido sguardo, è tutta piena
di lacrime nascoste.

Amore, gelosia, taciuta brama
di belle cose come prede esposte,
ti lasciano un rimpianto oscuro, aggiungono
ancora un filo nell'antica trama
che spezzerà, forse, la morte.

A galla ti riportano
non dettate virtù, ma d'altri accenti,
che un tremito confonde, la memoria.
La tua storia finisce, si nasconde . . .
Ma quanti cari cuori hai conquistati!

There, Now You Know

There, now you know our place is not
among the blessed; and that life,
like avid eyes, is full
of hidden tears.

Love, jealousy, unspoken lust
for things of beauty like defenseless prey,
leave behind a dark regret, add yet
another thread to the ancient weave
that death, perhaps, shall rend.

To the surface you are brought back
not by virtues learned, but by the memory
of other voices, that blur as you shudder.
Your story ends, drops out of sight.
Yet how many precious hearts you've won!

Partita

Quante speranze nel gioco! Ma poi,
sul tavolo abbattute,
tutte le carte erano contraries.

Fu il destino, e l'accetto. Non gli faccio
mal viso, non mi lagno
come nella chiassosa giovanezza.

Ma conosco la scala che all'altezza
conduce a me possibile.
               Mi levo
tra volti amici, conto il mio guadagno.

Game

I'd staked such hope in it! But then,
once they were laid on the table,
all the cards were against me.

It was fate. I accept it. I don't
scowl at it, I don't complain,
as I used to do in clamorous youth.

Yet I know what straight might lead up,
ladder-like, to myself.
                          I rise
among friendly faces, count my winnings.

Principio d'estate

Dolore, dove sei? Qui non ti vedo;
ogni apparenza t'è contraria. Il sole
indora la città, brilla nel mare.
D'ogni sorta veicoli alla riva
portano in giro qualcosa o qualcuno.
Tutto si muove lietamente, come
tutto fosse di esistere felice.

Beginning of Summer

Sorrow, where are you? I don't see you anywhere.
Appearances are all against you. The sun
sheds gold upon the city, shining on the sea.
Every kind of vehicle is carrying
someone or something to the coast.
Everything moves cheerfully, as if
all existence were meant to be happy.

Notte d'estate

Dalla stanza vicina ascolto care
voci nel letto dove il sonno accolgo.
Per l'aperta finestra un lume brilla,
lontano in cima al colle, chi sa dove.

Qui ti stringo al mio cuore, amore mio,
morto a me da infiniti anni oramai.

Summer Night

In the room next door I hear beloved
voices from my bed as I gather sleep.
A streetlamp shines through the open window,
far away, atop a hill, anywhere at all.

I clutch you to my breast, my love,
now dead to me for countless years.

Da quando

Da quando la mia bocca è quasi muta
amo le vite che quasi non parlano.
Un albero; ed appena—sosta dove
io sosto, la mia via riprende lieto—
il docile animale che mi segue.

Al giogo che gli è imposto si rassegna.
Una supplice occhiata, al più, mi manda.
Eterne verità, tacendo, insegna.

Ever Since

Ever since my tongue has fallen almost silent
I love those lives that almost do not speak.
A tree, or even the submissive animal
following behind me, stopping when I stop,
happy just to echo my existence.

He accepts the yoke assigned to him.
At most he'll give me an imploring glance.
In silence, he imparts eternal truths.

Per un fanciullo ammalato

Nella casa patema ti aggiravi
silenzioso come un gatto. Il nome
sapevi, non la realtà, del dolore.

Dai tuoi compagni diviso, le rose
sulle guance affilate impallidivano.

Rinato dalla mia anima, fiore
della vita, fanciullo amico. È tua
questa che ancora mi rimane estrema
lacrima che non vedi.

For a Sick Young Boy

You used to run about your father's house
silent as a cat. Pain you knew by name
alone, and not for what it really is.

Far from your companions, the roses
on your bony cheeks began to fade.

Dear young friend, flower of life,
reborn within my soul. It's yours,
this final, yet remaining tear
of mine, which you can't see.

Finestra

Il vuoto
del cielo sul color di purgatorio
delle tegole. Dietro, la materna
linea dei colli; in basso l'erta dove
dai cornicioni del teatro calano
i colombi; verdeggia
un albero che poca terra nutre;
statue portano alati sulla lira;
fanciulli con estrose grida vagano
in corsa.

Window

Empty
sky over purgatory-colored
tiles. In the distance, the hills'
maternal silhouette; below, a ramp
where pigeons flutter down from the roof
of the theatre; a tree
grows green in meager earth;
birds perch on statues' lyres;
children scream capriciously
running to and fro.

Fumo

Conforto delle lunghe insonni notti
d'inverno
       —allora in labirinti oscuri
errò, di angoscia, il pensiero; la mano
corse affannosa al tuo richiamo –
                il filo
tenue che sale, poi si rompe, il cielo,
dall'aperta finestra, di un suo raggio
colora;

e mi ricorda una casetta, sola
fra i campi, che fumava per la cena.

Smoke

Consolation of the long and sleepless nights
of winter
        —when the mind would wander
through dark labyrinths of anguish, the hand
come running breathless at your call—
                        the slender
wisp that rises, and then breaks, the sky
colors, through the open window, with
a beam;

it reminds me of a little house, alone
in the fields, smoking with the evening meal.

Prospettiva

La gente in fretta dirada.
                                    Filari
d'alberi nudi ai lati del viale,
in fondo là dove campagne sfumano,
si avvicinano—pare—in una stretta.
E v'entra un poco di quel cielo lilla
che turba e non consola.
                                    Breve sera,
troppo, in vista, tranquilla.

Perspective

People scatter in haste.
                              Rows
of leafless trees along the avenue,
in the distance where the land begins
to blur, seem to press and join together.
There a hint of lilac sky peers through,
ominous, unsettling.
                              Brief evening,
too peaceful to the eye.

Spettacolo

Tu non lasci deluso lo spettacolo
dove amori t'incantano e venture
e senti in quelle truccate figure
tutti i tuoi giovani sogni irritarsi.

Altre, quand'ero come te, ho versate
dolci usurpate lacrime.

Ora è tardi. Si spogliano le cose,
se ne tocca lo scheletro. Una veste
ancora piace, se bella. Più spesso
è la menzogna inutile, che annoia.

Performance

You do not leave the theatre disappointed.
Love-affairs and intrigues cast their spell,
your youthful dreams enflamed in all
those costumed figures on the stage.

Like you in another age, other
tender, stolen tears I wept.

It is late now. Things shed their clothing,
we touch them to the bone. A dress can still
please the eye, if beautiful. More often
the lie is pointless, irritating.

Rittatto

Lascia lo specchio. Non guardarti in quello
come una giovanetta. Che alle donne
è lume il corpo; a te l'animo vale.

La dolcezza che opponi ingenuo al male
fa la bontà del tuo sguardo. Ma il ciuffo
di capelli, che un po' butti in disparte,
d'esser te stesso la fierezza esprima,

come in cima a una casa già compiuta
la bandierta
che libera lassù s'agita a un vento.

Portrait

Never mind the mirror. Don't gaze in it
like some young girl. For women the body is
luminous; for you it's the mind that counts.

The charm with which you innocently fight the bad
gives your eyes their goodness. And yet the lock
of hair you lightly toss aside
is meant to flaunt the pride of being you,

like a banner atop a house
just finished,
flapping freely in the wind.

Una notte

Verrebbe il sonno come l'altre notti,
s'insinua già tra i miei pensieri.
                              Allora,
come una lavandaia un panno, torce
la nuova angoscia il mio cuore. Vorrei
gridare, ma non posso. La tortura,
che si soffre una volta, soffro muto.

Ahi, quello che ho perduto so io solo.

One Night

Sleep should come as any other night,
it's already slipping in between my thoughts.
                                        But

then, like a washerwoman with a cloth,
another anguish twists my heart. I want
to scream, but I cannot. Torture
we suffer but once. I suffer it voiceless.

Ah, I alone know what I've lost.

Porto

. . . A scordarla ancor m'aggiro
io per il porto, come un levantino.
(*Trieste e una donna*).

Qui dove imberbi scritturali il peso
registravano, e curvi sotto il carico
in fila indiana sudati braccianti
salivano scendevano oscillanti
scale dai moli agli alti bordi, preso
fra bestemmie e muggiti, della vita
solo un pensiero a me era nocente.

Cercavo a quello un angolo ridente.
Molti, all'ombra di pergole, ne aveva
la mia città inquieta. Mi premeva
isolarmi con lui, mettere assieme
versi, cavare dal suo male un bene.

Spero ancora un rifugio allo stratempo.
Ecco: è stato miracolo trovarlo.
Tutto, se chiedo, posso avere, fuori
quel mio cuore, quell'aria mia e quel tempo.

Port

. . . To forget her I still wander
about the port, like a Levantine.

(*Trieste and a Woman*)

Here where beardless clerks would register the weights
and sweaty stevedores, bent beneath their loads,
climbed up and down unsteady stairs in single
file between piers and ships' tall sides, amid
curses and bellowings, one thought alone
in life was dangerous to me.

I was looking for a friendly place for it.
And there were many, by the shade of arbors,
in my restless city. I had to be
alone with it, to put some lines together,
to glean some good from that unhappiness.

I'm still hoping for a shelter from the squalls.
There: by some miracle I've found one.
If I wish, I can have everything, except
that heart of mine, that air of mine, that time.

from 1944

Avevo

Da una burrasca ignobile approdato
a questa casa ospitale, m'affaccio
—liberamente alfine—alla finestra.
Guardo nel cielo nuvole passare,
biancheggiare lo spicchio della luna,

Palazzo Pitti di fronte. E mi volgo
vane antiche domande: Perché, madre,
m'hai messo al mondo? Che ci faccio adesso
che sono vecchio, che tutto s'innova,
che il passato è macerie, che alla prova
impari mi trovi di spaventose
vicende? Viene meno anche la fede
nella morte, che tutto essa risolva.

Avevo il mondo per me; avevo luoghi
del mondo dove mi salvavo. Tanta
luce in quelli ho veduto che, a momenti,
ero una luce io stesso. Ricordi,
tu dei miei giovani amici il più caro,
tu quasi un figlio per me, che non pure
se dove sei, né se piùsei, che a volte
progioniero ti penso nella terra
squallida, in mano al nemico? Vergogna
mi prende allora di quel poco cibo,
dell'ospitale provvisorio tetto.
Tutto mi portò via il fascista abbietto
ed il tedesco lurco.

Avevo una famiglia, una compagna;
la buona, la meravigliosa Lina.
È viva ancora, ma al riposo inclina
più che i suoi anni impongano. Ed un'ansia
pietà mi prende di vederla ancora,
in non sue case affaccendata, il fuoco
alimentare a scarse legna. D'altri
tempi al ricordo doloroso il cuore
si stringe, come ad un rimorso, in petto.
Tutto mi portò via il fascista abbietto
ed il tedesco lurco.

I Used to Have

Driven by a shameful storm
to this sheltering home, I can
finally, freely, look out the window.
I see clouds pass in the sky,
the crescent moon shining white,

Palazzo Pitti across the way. I ask myself
the age-old useless questions. Why, mother,
did you bring me into the world? What am I to do
here now that I am old and all is being remade,
now that the past is only rubble and, when
put to the test, I find myself unequal to the terrible
events? Even my faith in death, as
the resolution of all, now fails me.

I used to have the world to myself, and
places in it to which I could escape. So much
light did I see there that at times
I, too, became a light. Do you remember,
you, the dearest of my young friends,
so like a son to me? I don't even know
now where you are, or if you are; at times
I imagine you a prisoner in the land
of gloom, in enemy hands. And at such moments
I feel ashamed of my paltry meals
and the roof that shelters me for now.
The fascists and the Germans
took everything away from me.

I used to have a family and a wife,
the good, the wondrous Lina.
She's still alive, but tends to weary
more than age would warrant. A
terrible pity grips me still to see her
busy in houses not her own, stoking
fires with insufficient wood. Thinking
back with sorrow on the past, I feel
my heart ache, as if in remorse.
The fascists and the Germans
took everything away from me.

Avevo una bambina, oggi una donna.
Di me vedevo in lei la miglior parte.
Tempo funesto anche trovava l'arte
di staccarla da me che la radice
vede in me dei suoi mali, né più l'occhio
mi volge, azzurro, con l'usato affetto.
Tutto mi portò via il fascista abbietto
ed il tedesco lurco.

Avevo una città bella tra i monti
rocciosi e il mare luminoso. Mia
perché vi nacqui, più che d'altri mia
che la scoprivo fanciullo, ed adulto
per sempre a Italia la sposai col canto.
Vivere si doveva. Ed io per tanto
scelsi fra i mali il più degno: fu il piccolo
d'antichi libri raro negozietto.
Tutto mi portò via il fascista inetto
ed il tedesco lurco.

Avevo un cimitero ove mia madre
riposa, e i vecchi di mia madre. Bello
come un giardino; e quante volte in quello
mi rifugiavo col pensiero! Oscuri
esigli e lunghi, atre vicende, dubbio
quel giardino mi mostrano e quel letto.
Tutto mi portò via il fascista abbietto
—anche la tomba—ed il tedesco lurco.

I used to have a little girl, now a woman.
In her I saw the best of me.
Dreaded time has found a way
to drive her, too, from me, and now she sees
me as the root of her misfortunes, and no longer
casts her blue eyes on me with the same affection.
The fascists and the Germans
took everything away from me.

I used to have a beautiful city between
rocky hills and a glistening sea. She was mine
because I was born there, more mine than anyone's
because I found her when a boy and as a man
I married her to Italy forever with song.
But one has to live, and so I chose
the least unworthy evil as my own:
a splendid little shop of old, rare books.
The fascists and the Germans
took everything away from me.

I used to have a cemetery, where
my mother and her forebears rest. It was
pretty as a garden. How often I would flee
there with my thoughts! Long, uncertain
exiles, and other things as well, and doubt,
that garden, that bed, brought back to me.
The fascists and the Germans
took everything—the very grave—away from me.

Teatro degli Artigianelli

Falce martello e la stella d'Italia
ornano nuovi la sala. Ma quanto
dolore per quel segno su quel muro!

Entra, sorretto dalle grucce, il Prologo.
Saluta al pugno; dice sue parole
perché le donne ridano e i fanciulli
che affollano la povera platea.
Dice, timido ancora, dell'idea
che gli animi affratella; chiude: "E adesso
faccio come i tedeschi: mi ritiro."
Tra un atto e l'altro, alla Cantina, in giro
rosseggia parco ai bicchieri l'amico
dell'uomo, cui rimargina ferite,
gli chiude solchi dolorosi; alcuno
venuto qui da spaventosi esigli,
si scalda a lui come chi ha freddo al sole.

Questo è il Teatro degli Artigianelli,
quale lo vide il poeta nel mille
novecentoquarantaquattro, un giorno
di Settembre, che a tratti
rombava ancora il cannone, e Firenze
taceva, assorta nelle sue rovine.

Workman's Theatre

Hammer, sickle, star of Italy,
all brand new, adorn the hall. Such sorrow,
though, for that sign on that wall!

In comes the Prologue, on crutches. He gives
a clenched fist salute. He says some things
to make the women and children laugh
from the crowded floor before him.
He speaks still timidly of the idea
that brings them all together, concluding
"Now I'll make like the Germans and withdraw."
Between acts, in the Cantina, spare
and flowing red in tumblers, man's friend
makes the rounds, healing wounds, closing
painful chasms; some, having come here
from terrible exiles, warm themselves with it
as a freezing man warms himself in the sun.

This is the Workman's Theatre,
as the poet saw it in nineteen
hundred forty-four, on a September
day when now and then the guns
still rumbled, and Florence lay
silent, rapt in her ruins.

from

VARIE

MISCELLANY

(undated)

Privilegio

Io sono un buon compagno. Agevolmente
mi si prende per mano, e quello faccio
ch'altri mi chiede, bene e lietamente.

Ma l'anima secreta che non mente
a se stessa mormora sue parole.
Anche talvolta un dio mi chiama, e vuole
ch'io l'ascolti. Ai pensieri
che mi nascono allora, al cuor che batte
dentro, all'intensità del mio dolore,
ogni uguaglianza fra gli uomini spengo.

Ho questo privilegio. E lo mantengo.

Privilege

I am a good companion. One easily
takes me by the hand, and I do well
and gladly what others ask of me.

But the hidden soul, which does not lie
to itself, whispers when it speaks.
At times, in fact, a god calls out to me
and bids me listen. And by the thoughts
that fill me then, by the heart that beats
in me, by the sharpness of the pain I feel,
I suspend all equality among men.

That is my privilege. And I intend to keep it.

from

MEDITERRRANEE

MEDITERRANEA

(1945-1946)

Due antiche favole

1   IL RATTO DI GANIMEDE

Era un giorno fra i giorni. Era sereno
l'Ida; le capre brucavano in pace,
date in guardia a pastore adolescente.
Solo il cane qua e là vagava inquieto.

Sul volto del fanciullo ombre passavano.
Forse troppo severo il re suo padre.
Forse anelava ai compagni
                                            —sull'Ida
erano molti della stessa età,

che tutti delle stesse gare amanti,
per il bacio di un serto, violenti
si abbracciavano a un coro d'alte grida.—
Bianche in cielo correvano le nubi.

Sempre il cane su e giù fiutava all'erta,
ed il gregge più unito in sé stringevasi.
Ai presagi insensibile, il pastore,
oblioso al suo compito, sognava.
Fulminava dal cielo aquila fosca.
Si sbandavano greggi, si sgolava
il cane.
            Già dell'azzurro il fanciullo
bagnava un'ultima volta la terra.

Two Ancient Fables

1   THE RAPE OF GANYMEDE

It was a day like any other. Mount Ida
stood serene, the goats grazing placidly,
tended by their adolescent guardian.
Only the dog ran to and fro, uneasy.

Shadows fell over the young boy's face.
Perhaps his father, the king, was too severe.
Perhaps he yearned for his companions
                      —many

on Ida were the same age as he,

all enamoured of the same games, where
for a laurel's kiss they used to clutch
each other fiercely to a chorus of shouts.—
The clouds raced white across the sky.

The dog still sniffed about warily,
the flock pressed more tightly together.
Unmindful of the omens, forgetful of
his duties, the goatherd boy was dreaming.
From the heavens flashed the sullen eagle.
The flocks dispersed, the dog barked
and barked.
           But the boy was of the sky already
and sprinkled the earth for the last time.

2 NARCISO AL FONTE

Quando giunse Narciso al suo destino
—dai pastori deserto e dalle greggi
nell'ombra di un boschetto azzurro fonte—
subito si chinò sullo specchiante.

Oh, il bel volto adorabile!
                              Le frondi
importune scostò, cercò la bocca
che cercava la sua viva anelante.
Il bacio che gli rese era di gelo.
Sbigottì. Ritornò al suo cieco errore.

Perché caro agli dèi si mutò in fiore
bianco sulla sua tomba.

2 NARCISSUS AT THE POOL

When Narcissus found his destiny
—an azure pool yet undisturbed by shepherds
and their flocks, in the cool shade of a grove—
he looked down at once into the mirroring.

Oh, the beauty of that face!
                                    Brushing
aside some branches in the way, he sought
the mouth that sought out his same living, breathless one.
And the kiss it gave him was of ice.
He faltered, then repeated his blind mistake.

Beloved of the gods, he turned into a flower,
white upon his grave.

Angelo

O tu che contro me vecchio nel fiore
dei tuoi anni ti levi, occhi che all'ira
fiammeggiano più nostra come stelle,
bocca che ai baci dati e ricevuti
armonizzi parole, è forse il mio
incauto amarti un sacrilegio? Or questo
è fra me e Dio.

Alto cielo! Mio bel splendente amore!

Angel

O you who in the bloom of youth rise up
against the old man that I am, with eyes
that burn like stars with the most human wrath,
a mouth that with the kisses given and received
should turn words into music—is my reckless
loving you perhaps a sacrilege? That is
between God and me.

Heavens above!
My great, resplendent love!

Mediterranea

Penso un mare lontano, un porto, ascose
vie di quel porto; quale un giorno v'ero,
e qui oggi sono, che agli dèi le palme
supplice levo, non punirmi vogliano
di un'ultima vittoria che depreco
(ma il cuore, per dolcezza, regge appena);

penso cupa sirena
—baci ebbrezza delirio—; penso Ulisse
che si leva laggiù da un triste letto.

Mediterranea

I see a distant sea, a port, its hidden
streets. As I was there once,
and am here now, palms raised in supplication
to the gods, let them not punish me
for one last victory I do not want
(by my love, I've barely the heart for it);

I see a somber siren
—drunken kisses and delirium—I see Ulysses
rising from a gloomy bed.

Raccontino

La casa è devastata,
la casa è rovinata.
Mille e una notte non l'abita più .

Come un giardino la sua verde Aleppo
una tenera madre ricordava.
Accoglieva le amiche, palpitava
per il figlio inquieto. Ed il caffè
porgeva, in piccole tazze, alla turca.

La casa è. devastate,
la casa è rovinata.
Mille e una notte non accoglie più .

La rovinò dal cielo
la guerra,
in terra
la devastava il tedesco. Piangeva
la gentile le proprie sue e le umane
miserie. (Odiare non poteva). Il figlio
fuggì sui monti, vi trovò un suo caro
amico, vi giocò con lui la vita.

Erano cari amici, si facevano
meraviglia a vicenda, esageravano,
un poco invidiosi, donne amori.
Erano cari amid quando rompere
tu li vedevi esterrefatto a calci:
un'antilope e un mulo.

La casa è devastata,
la casa è rovinata.
Ma i due ragazzi sono vivi ancora;
vive ancora, imbianchite un po', le madri.

Very Short Story

The house is destroyed,
the house is in ruins.
The Arabian nights live there no more.

A loving mother talked about
her green Aleppo as a garden.
She was entertaining friends,
fretting for her restless son. And the coffee
she poured out, in little cups, was Turkish.

The house is destroyed,
the house is in ruins.
The Arabian nights entertain no more.

The war from the sky
destroyed it;
the Germans by land
left it in ruins. The lady
bewailed her own afflictions and those
of all the world. (She could never hate.) Her son
had fled to the mountains, and there found
an old friend, risking his life at his side.

They were close friends and liked
to impress each other, exaggerating loves
and women, a little to the other's envy.
They were still friends when to your horror
you saw them kicking like a mule and antelope,
the day their friendship ended.

The house is destroyed,
the house is in ruins.
The boys are still alive,
the mothers too, a little greyer.

Tre poesie a Telemaco

1   QUASI UNA FAVOLA

Tutti portiamo della vita il peso,
in ogni luogo, in ogni tempo nati.

Ma il giovane stornello in cui ponevo
qualche speranza d'avvenire, e il cuore
lasciava pegno a un'ochetta, ben giura
che v'è al mondo un paese—agli altri in odio
fortissimo paese—ove il migliore
sempre vince, e per tutti è bene nascere.

Odo, se veglio la notte, lamenti
del ragazzo nel sonno; odo nel sonno
sussulti d'anime in pena. E al risveglio
ogni volto s'oscura.

Three Poems to Telemachus

1   ALMOST A FABLE

We all must bear life's burdens,
whenever, wherever we are born.

But the young starling in whom I placed
some hope for the future, having pledged
my heart to a goose, firmly swears that
in this world there is a land—very strong
and hated by the rest—where the best
man always wins, and all are born to happiness.

At night, when awake, I hear the young boy
groaning in his sleep; when asleep, I hear
the gasps of souls in torment. And when I wake
all faces darken.

"Se non era l'Italia il tuo paese
—dico per dire: lo so ben che l'ami—
quale ti garberebbe patria?" Io taccio;
egli ripete la domanda.—"E tu?"

Mi guarda coi suoi grande occhi che toccano
per dolcezza dell'anima i confini
materni; forma un nome la sua bocca
come un bacio. Pensoso, io nulla dico.

Ecco il suo volto al mio silenzio farsi
severo, gli occhi a un odio scintillanti.
Non fosse che pietà rispetto accoglie
dei più vecchi di lui, di lui garanti,
su me si getterebe, io penso, come
sopra un nemico.

2 METAMORPHOSIS

"If Italy were not your country
—just supposing; I know how much you
love it—where would you like to live?" I am
silent. He repeats the question . . . . "And you?"

He looks at me with great big eyes
that in their sweetness touch the soul's
maternal confines. His lips begin to form
a name like a kiss. Pensive, I say nothing.

And at my silence then his face turns harsh,
his eyes begin to flash with hatred.
If not for the respect that pity grants him
towards his elders, his guardians,
I think he'd hurl himself at me
as at an enemy.

3   APPENA UNA CITAZIONE

Dici che lei ti lasciava, che solo
porti la pena d'esser nato. *Un'ombra,*
inseguo a lungo per vie solitarie,
a un barlume di luce dei fanali,
per sempre chiusa nella mia memoria.

Penso che i versi sono belli. E forse,
l'ombra inseguendo, troverai un corpo.

Un dolce corpo ti consolerà.

3   ALMOST A QUOTATION

You say she's left you now, and all alone
you bear the pain of being alive. I follow
a shadow far along deserted streets,
to a glimmer of light from the lampposts,
forever closed within my memory.

The lines are good, I think. And perhaps,
by following the shadow, you'll find a body.

A sweet body to console you.

Ulisse

Nella mia giovanezza ho navigato
lungo le coste dalmate. Isolotti
a fior d'onda emergevano, ove raro
un uccello sostava intento a prede,
coperti d'alghe, scivolosi, al sole
belli come smeraldi. Quando l'alta
marea e la notte li annullava, vele
sottovento sbandavano più al largo,
per fuggirne l'insidia. Oggi il mio regno
è quella terra di nessuno. Il porto
accende ad altri i suoi lumi; me al largo
sospinge ancora il non domato spirito,
e della vita il doloroso amore.

Ulysses

In my youth I sailed along the rough coasts
of Dalmatia. Just above the surface
of the waves the little islands rose, algae-
covered, slippery, bright as emeralds in the sun,
landings for the occasional bird
intently seeking prey. When at high tide
and at night they disappeared, all leeward sails
would heel out far towards the open sea,
fleeing their danger. Today my kingdom
is that no-man's land. For other men the port
now lights its lamps; while out to sea I still
am driven by a spirit unsubdued,
and by a painful love of life itself.

from

EPIGRAFE

EPIGRAPH

(1947-48)

Per una favola nuova

Ogni anno un passo avanti e il mondo dieci
indietro. Al fine son rimasto solo.

Ma tu mi rendi il perduto, usignolo
che sul mio ramo ti posi, e la storia
narri per me dell'angelo che vive
due giorni e mezzo sulla terra. Scrive
la tua mano inesperta, e fa che intorno
alla favola nuova i miei pensieri
sciamano assidui come api al miele.

Accusi l'arte difficile e gelo
la parola all'immagine. Ed io penso
che sei più dei tuoi anni giovinetto;
che chi presto matura (è antico detto)
manca in breve al suo stelo.

Toward a New Fable

Every year it's one step forward, ten steps
back for everybody else. And in the end I'm left alone.

But what I've lost you give me back, nightingale
alighting on my branch. You tell me
of the angel who for two days and a half
came down on earth to live. You
write with an unpracticed hand, and make
my thoughts come swarming round your fable
avid as the bees that fly to honey.

Art you spurn as difficult; I freeze
the word in images. And I think
that you are younger than your years,
and that he who grows up early (it's an
old saying) does not long elude the grave.

from

UCCELLI

BIRDS

(1948)

L'ornitologo pietoso

Raccolse un ornitologo pietoso
un espulso dal nido. Come l'ebbe
in mano vide ch'era un rosignuolo.

In salvo lo portò con il timore
gli mancasse per via. Gli fece, a un fondo
di fiasco, un nido; ritrovò quel gramo
l'imbeccata e il calore. Fu allevarlo
cura non lieve, ed il dispendio certo
di molte uova di formiche. E ai giorni
sereni, ai prima gorgheggi, l'esperto
in un boschetto libertà gli dava.
"più—diceva al perduto, e lo guardava
a terra e in ramo cercarsi—il tuo grazie
udrò sommesso" E si sentì più solo.

The Kindly Ornithologist

A kindly ornithologist rescued
a fledgling driven from the nest. In his hand
he saw it was a nightingale.

He carried it to safety, fearing it might
die along the way. From the bottom of a flask
he made a nest for it, and there the wretch
found food and warmth. Raising a bird
is not an easy task, and surely cost
him many ant-eggs. When fair weather
came, and with it the first warblings, the doctor
set it free in a small thicket. "Soon,"
he said to that lost soul, watching it
hop on the ground in search of a branch, "I'll
barely hear your tune of thanks." And he felt more alone.

Passeri

Saltellano sui tetti
passeri cinguettanti. Due si rubano
di becco il pane che ai leggeri sbricioli,
che carpire s'illudono al balcone.
Vanno a stormi a dormire . . .
                                    Uccelli sono:
nella Natura la sublimazione
del rettile.

Sparrows

About the rooftops hop
the chirping sparrows. Two of them
attempt to steal some bread from one another's beak,
to snatch in vain crumbs fallen on the balcony.

Off they go in flocks to sleep . . .

                                        They are birds:

Nature's sublimation
of the reptile.

Nietzsche

Intorno a una grandezza solitaria
non volano gli uccelli, né quei vaghi
gli fanno, accanto, il nido. Altro non odi
che il silenzio, non vedi altro che l'aria.

Nietzsche

Birds don't fly around a solitary
greatness, nor do they build their nests
nearby. All you ever hear there is
silence, all you ever see is air.

from

QUASI UN RACCONTO

ALMOST A STORY

(1951)

Passioni

Sono fatte di lacrime e di sangue
e d'altro ancora. Il cuore
batte a sinistra.

Passions

Are made of tears and blood
and many other things. The heart
beats on the left.

Dialogo

LUI

Di me diranno, quando sarò morto:
Povero vecchio disperato e solo:
Cantava come canta un rosignuolo.

LEI

Non sei un rosignuolo; sei un merlo.
Fischi piùforte la sera; e nessuno
può strapparti di becco il tuo pinolo.

Dialogue

HE:

When I'm dead they'll say of me:
Poor wretched old man, all alone.
He sang just like a nightingale.

SHE:

You're not a nightingale. You're a blackbird.
You chirp louder in the evening. And
No one can wrest the nut from your beak.

from

SEI POESIE DELLA VECCHIARIA

SIX POEMS OF OLD AGE

(1953-54)

Il poeta e il conformista

Come t'invidio, amico! Alla tua fede
saldamente ancorato, in pace vivi
con gli uomini e gli dei. Discorri scrivi
agevole, conforme volontà
del tuo padrone. In cambio egli ti dà
pane e, quale sua cosa, ti accarezza.
Arma non ti si appunta. E passi,
tra gli uomini e gli eventi, quasi illeso.

V'ha chi solo si pensa ed indifeso.
Pensa che la sua carne ha un buon sapore.
Meglio—pensa—chi è in vista al cacciatore
passero che pernice.

The Poet and the Conformist

How I envy you, my friend! Firmly
anchored in your faith, you live at peace
with gods and men. You speak and write
with ease, your will at one with your
master's. In return he gives you bread
and, as with his dog, he pats you on the head.
No weapon will he ever raise against you:
your smile dispels every threat. And so through life
and its events you pass almost unscathed.

Then there's the man who thinks himself alone
and defenseless. He thinks his flesh must taste good.
Better, in the hunter's sights—he thinks—
to be a sparrow than a partridge

I vecchi

I vecchi dei villaggi hanno (se l'hanno)
il tabacco. Hanno il vino rosso. A pochi
passi il temuto cimitero. Ed io
(non quello temo, ai vinti unico pio)
avrei dovuto guarire, sottrarmi
un farmaco letale, carcarimi
di pesi sempre piùgravi (ed è questa
—lo so—la legge della vita); darmi
promettevano in cambio, essi, una festa;

essi, i miei buoni amici. Perché tutto
ti concedono i buoni, e non la morte.

Old People

The old people in the villages have tobacco
(when they have it). They have red wine. And, a few steps
away, the dreaded cemetery. Whereas I
(who fear not that, sole comfort of the vanquished)
was supposed to get better, to avoid
all poisonous medications, to keep shouldering
ever heavier burdens (which is, I
know, the law of life). And in return
they promised me a party in my honor.

They, my good friends, that is. For the good
will grant you anything, except death.

Notes to the Poems

My Foster Mother's House

Saba's *nutrice*, which in Italian can mean both "wet nurse" and "foster mother," was Gioseffa Sabaz (or Schobar, depending on the source), a Slovenian Catholic woman who in fact was both wet-nurse and then foster-mother to the poet, for the first four years of his life. Saba was entrusted to her care, and that of her husband, immediately after his birth, since his legitimate father (whom he would not meet for another 21 years) was in jail at the time, never to return to the family, and his mother, financially destitute and despondent, was in no position to raise the child. In a letter dated September 18, 1955, Saba writes to Nora Baldi that as a newborn, "when someone would try to cover me, my mother would protest, saying that if I lived, I lived, and if I died, I died" (letter quoted in *Cronologia*, Saba, *Tutte le Poesie*, Arrigo Stara ed., Milan 1994). As the Schobars had just lost their only child, they welcomed "little Berto" into their home. For Saba, these early years of childhood, as we see even in this youthful poem, would forever serve as his model of happiness, a kind of lost paradise on earth, never to be regained. His poetry is full of echoes of this half-remembered state of grace. Saba's separation from "Peppa" (as Gioseffa was called) at age four, when his mother took him back into her own family, to be raised by her and zia Regina, was particularly traumatic (see the poems from "Little Berto," pp.____).

The Pig

This poem was originally published in Saba's second collection, *Coi miei occhi* ("With My Own Eyes," 1912), which contained the group of poems now called *Casa e campagna* ("House and Country") and some of those that make up *Trieste e una donna* ("Trieste and a Woman"). While later reprinted in some of the early editions of the Canzoniere, it ultimately was deleted from the definitive edition and only included, finally, in the *Canzoniere apocrifo*. Since it well complements the animal motif running through all of Saba's oeuvre, and since he expressed some regret, in the *History and Chronicle*, over having left it out of the *Canzoniere*, I have taken the liberty of including it in this

Songbook.

Autobiography, 4

The "pit" in which the poet sees himself in line 13 is, in the Italian, a *bolgia*, a word with obvious Dantean echoes, even in most of its colloquial uses. In Dante, a *bolgia* is one of the ten "pits" or "ditches" of the 8th circle of Hell.

Autobiography, 15

Lines 7-8—"he practices his honest, happy art, / with thoughts of Love, in solitude, unknown"; ("la sua opera compie, onesta e lieta, / d'Amor pensoso, ignoto e solitario")—clearly echo line 5 of Petrarch CCLXXIX: là'v'io seggia d'amor pensoso e scriva ("where I sit with thoughts of love and write.") That Saba chose, in the last sonnet of his *Autobiography,* to echo a poem of great solitude, written after Laura's death, late in Petrarch's life, serves to reconfirm his own sense of loneliness and "oldness" (he had always felt older than his years, and was only around 40 when he wrote this). Line 7, with its "honest, happy art," also echoes his own 1911 essay on poetics, "The Remaining Task of Poets" (published only posthumously), which is, in fact, to write "honest poetry."

THE PRISONERS

These poems, as Saba obliquely mentions in the *History and Chronicle,* are inspired by Michelangelo's so-called "Prisoners" (also sometimes called "Slaves"), a group of mostly (at least apparently) unfinished sculptures that represent human figures that look as if they are struggling to emerge from the marble blocks in which they are "imprisoned." The "Man of Lust" is modeled after one of the "finished" works of the group, the so-called "Dying Slave" now in the Louvre (cf. *History and Chronicle,* pp.___).

The Genius

The person speaking in this poem, according to Saba in the *History and Chronicle,* was loosely modeled on Michelangelo himself.

The Lover

The son of immortal Theseus is, of course, Hippolytus, who spurned the carnal love of Phaedra for the sake of his chaste, transcendent love of Artemis. But Saba appears to have playfully worked another speaker into the voice of this poem: Dante, especially the Dante of *La Vita Nuova*. The apostrophe "o gentile" is straight from the Florentine poet's early lyric work, and the chaste, young Dante, who certainly found his "victory palm" in Beatrice, might well have said, had he written in a modern tongue: "I love a woman whose bed I've not shared / and will never share, who knows nothing / of my love, on whom I scarcely dare to look."

Waking Up

Bolaffio is the painter Vittorio Bolaffio, a friend of Saba mentioned in several other poems of the *Canzoniere* (not included in this collection). The poem "La Brama" ("Desire," also not included here) is dedicated to him.

Three Cities, III. Florence

Montale's "generous gloom" refers to the poet's grim but committed antifascism, which Saba shared with him, whence the poems final's optimism.

Ever Since

The first lines of this poem, writes Saba as Carimandrei in the *History and Chronicle*, contain a "veiled reference" to the antisemitic "racial laws" passed in Italy in 1938, which "prohibited the publication of writings by Jews or those believed to be Jews, either in newspapers, magazines or books. For Saba, however, a relative exception was made. Magazines such as *Tempo*, *Prospettive*, *Corrente* and others whose names now escape me, welcomed, even solicited his poems. The publisher Arnoldo Mondadori, who wanted at the time to publish the Canzoniere, went personally to Rome to obtain authorization to do so. He

wasn't granted it, but Saba was grateful to him just the same..."
(see *History and Chronicle*, p._____). It is, at least in part,
because of the "relative exception" made for Saba that he says his
tongue has fallen "almost" silent. Matters would, of course, wors-
en considerably in 1943, when the Mussolini government fell
and German forces occupied the peninsula. Saba lost his bookshop and was forced to go into hiding.

1944

Written during the period when he was hiding from the German
authorities in Florence during the Occupation, this poem represents, in Saba's own terms, a "return" to the old, explicit manner,
after the more concentrated, elliptical poetry of *Words* and *Last
Things*. Saba's invocation, in the refrain, of *il tedesco lurco* ("the
swilling German") is a Dantean reminiscence: *e come là tra li
tedeschi lurchi / lo bivero s'assetta a far sua guerra* ("and as there
among the swilling Germans / the beaver settles in to wage his
war"; Inf., XVII, 21-22). Since this echo would not be so immediately apparent in English, and since the refrain to me sounded
more effective, in its starkness, without any adjectives at all, "the
abject Fascist and the swilling German" have become, in my
translation, simply "the Fascists and the Germans." For more on
this poem, see the *History and Chronicle*, pp. _____.

Select Bibliography

Works by Umberto Saba

First editions:

Poesie. Preface by Silvio Benco, Florence, Casa Editrice Italiana, 1911.

Coi miei occhi (Il mio secondo libro di versi). Florence, Libreria della Voce, 1912

Cose leggere e vaganti. Trieste, La Libreria Antica e Moderna, 1920.

Il Canzoniere, 1900-1921. Trieste, La Libreria Antica e Moderna, 1921.

Preludio e canzonette. Turin, Edizioni di "Primo Tempo", 1923.

Figure e canti. Milan, Ed. Fratelli Treves, 1926.

L'Uomo. Trieste, 1926.

Preludio e fughe. Florence, Edizioni di Solaria, 1928.

Tre Poesie alla mia balia. Trieste, 1929.

Ammonizione ed altre poesie. 1900-1910, Trieste, 1932.

Tre composizioni. Preceded by an Appendix to "Figure e canti," Milan-Rome, Treves-Treccani-Tumminelli, Ed. Fratelli Treves, 1933.

Parole. Lanciano, R. Carabba editore, 1934.

Ultime cose (1935-1938). Preface by Gianfranco Contini, Lugano, Collana di Lugano, 1944.

Il Canzoniere (1900-1945). Rome, Einaudi, 1945.

Mediterranee. Milan, Mondadori, 1946.

Storia e cronistoria del Canzoniere. Milan, Mondadori, 1948.

Uccelli. Trieste, Edizioni dello Zibaldone, 1950.

Uccelli - Quasi un racconto (1948-1951). Milan, Mondadori, 1951 ("Tutte le Opere" XIV).

Epigrafe - Ultime Prose. With two drawings by Renato Guttuso and one by Carlo Levi, preface by Giacomo Debenedetti, Milan, Il Saggiatore, 1959.

Quello che resta da fare ai poeti. Edizioni dello Zibaldone, Trieste, 1959.

Prose. Mondadori, Milan, 1964.

Editions of the *Canzoniere*:

Il Canzoniere (1900-1945). Rome, Einaudi, 1945.
Il Canzoniere (1900-1947). 2nd edition, expanded and revised, Turin, Einaudi, 1948.
Il Canzoniere (1900-1947). Third edition, Turin, Einaudi, 1957.
Il Canzoniere (1900-1947). Fourth edition, Turin, Einaudi, 1958.
Il Canzoniere (1900-1954). Fifth edition, Turin, Einaudi, 1961.
Il Canzoniere (1900-1954). Sixth edition, Turin, Einaudi, 1965.
Il Canzoniere 1981. Critical edition, Giordano Castellani, ed., Milan, Fondazione Arnoldo e Alberto Mondadori, 1981.

Tutte le poesie. Arrigo Stara, ed., Introduction by Mario Lavagetto, Mondadori, Milan, 1988 (1994).

Anthologies of the *Canzoniere*;

Antologia del Canzoniere. Carlo Muscetta, ed., Turin, Einaudi, 1963.

Poesie scelte. Giovanni Giudici ed., with a bio-bibliographical note by Sergio Miniussi, Milan, Mondadori, 1976.

Il Canzoniere. Selection edited by Folco Portinari, Turin, Einaudi, 1976.

Per conoscere Saba. Mario Lavagetto ed., Milan, Mondadori, 1981.

Coi miei occhi. Claudio Milanini ed., Milan, Il Saggiatore, 1981.

Saba in English

The Promised Land, and Other Poems. An Anthology of Four Contemporary Italian Poets: Umberto Saba, Giuseppe Ungaretti, Eugenio Montale and Salvatore Quasimodo; Sergio Pacifici, ed., S.F. Vanni, N.Y, 1957.

318

SELECTION OF POEMS PUBLISHED BY CARCANET, INFO
TO BE PROVIDED

Umberto Saba: An Anthology of his Poetry and Criticism. Selected and
translated by Robert Harrison. International Book Publishers, Troy,
Michigan, 1986.

Ernesto. Translated by Mark Thompson, New York, Carcanet, 1987.

The Stories and Recollections of Umberto Saba. Translated by Estelle
Gilson, Sheep Meadow Press, Riverdale, 1993.

Critical and Biographical works on Saba

Anceschi, Luciano, Poetiche del novecento in Italia, Turin, Paravia
1962 (1972).

Aymone, Renato, Saba e la psicanalisi. Naples, Guida 1971.

Baldi, Nora, Il paradiso di Saba. Milan, Mondadori, 1958.

Caccia, Ettore, Lettura e storia di Saba. Milan, Bietti, 1967.

Cecchi, Ottavio, L'aspro vino di Saba. Rome, Editori Riuniti, 1994.

Cary, Joseph, *Three Modern Italian Poets: Saba, Ungaretti, Montale.*
University of Chicago Press, 1993 (2nd ed.).

Ferri, Teresa, Poetica e stile di Umberto Saba. Urbino, Edizioni
Quattro Venti, 1984.

Guagnini, Enrico, Il punto su Saba, Rome-Bari, Laterza, 1987.

Lavagetto, Mario, La Gallina di Saba. Turin, Einaudi, 1974.

Morandini, Luciano, L'orologio di Saba. Udine, Caampanotto, 1994.

Muzzioli, Francesco, ed., La Critica e Saba. Bologna, Cappelli, 1976.

Portinari, Folco, Umberto Saba. Milan, Mursia, 1963.

Raimondi, Pietro, Invito alla lettura di Saba. Milan, Mursia, 1974-
78.

Rella, Franco, La cognizione del male: Saba e Montale. Rome, Editori
Riuniti, 1985.

Biographical Note

STEPHEN SARTARELLI's publications include *Grievances and Other Poems* (Gnosis Press, 1989) and *Phantasmatikon* (Alea Chapbooks, 1992). Hr has translated the French classics *Voyage Around My Room*, by Xavier de Maistre (New Directions, 1994) and *The Devil in Love*, by Jacques Cazotte (Marsilio, 1993), as well as contemporary Italian novels such as T*he Plague Sower*, by Gesualdo Bufalino (Eridanos, 1989). His poems, translations and articles have also appeared in a wide variety of periodicals.

Yehuda Amichai
Great Tranquility: Questions and Answers
Translated by Glenda Abramson and Tudor Parfitt

Poems of Jerusalem and Love Poems
Translated by Yehuda Amichai, Ted Hughes, Stephen Mitchell and others

The Early Books of Yehuda Amichai
Translated by Harold Schimmel, Ted Hughes, Assia Gutmann, and Yehuda Amichai

Yona Wallach
Wild Light
Translated by Linda Zisquit

Allen Afterman
Kabbalah and Consciousness

Dennis Silk
Plays, Puppet Plays and Theater Writings

Khaled Mattawa
Ismailia Eclipse

F.T. Prince
Collected Poems 1935-1992
Walks in Rome

David Jones
The Roman Quarry

Christopher Middleton
Intimate Chronicles

John Peck
Agura
Poems and Translations of Hi-Lo

Stanley Kunitz
Interviews and Encounters with Stanley Kunitz
A Celebration for Stanley Kunitz

Diana Der-Hovanessian
Any Day Now
Selected Poems
The Circle Dancers

Mary Kinzie
Summers of Vietnam